The HerStories

Project

The HerStories Project

WOMEN EXPLORE THE JOY, PAIN, AND POWER OF FEMALE FRIENDSHIP

JESSICA SMOCK AND STEPHANIE SPRENGER

HSP PRESS

THE HERSTORIES PROJECT: WOMEN EXPLORE THE JOY, PAIN, AND POWER OF FEMALE FRIENDSHIP

Copyright 2013 by Jessica Smock and Stephanie Sprenger

ISBN: 978-1-49375-297-3

Printed in the United States of America

Dedication

To Gavin and Adrian, Janice, Lucas, Hannah, Kelly, Billy, Madison, Hallie, Logan, and Emma – JS
To my mom for teaching me so much about the powerful bonds between women, to my daughters, Izzy and Sophie, and to the tribe of girlfriends I rely on to keep me sane. –SCS

Contents

What's Old: Family Ties and Early Friendships

What's Changed: Tales of Motherhood and Friendship

What's Lost: Friendship Breakups and Losses

Foreword

Jill Smokler

My best friend got married last spring.

The two of us spent our childhoods planning our weddings together, and she stood beside me as maid of honor 13 years ago at my own nuptials. She was a vision in white on her own wedding day, the California sea a perfect backdrop to her exuberance. Her brother, whom I watched grow up from a precious tow-headed toddler into a grown man, lovingly officiated the ceremony. The flowers were exactly as she always planned and her father beamed as he walked her down the aisle. It was a *perfect* day.

Unfortunately, I watched it all unfold on Facebook from 3,000 miles away.

We said we'd never let it happen again. After years of intermittent junior high and high school estrangements over silly misunderstandings and wounded feelings, we were once again as close as sisters. She acted as godparent to my children and I provided an endless shoulder for her fears of never finding "the one." She accompanied us on summer vacations, and Halloween became a tradition she never missed. My children didn't understand how they could have an "aunt" if I didn't have a sister, but no other title would be fitting for her.

But as all parents know, priorities change when you have children, and so do friendships. My love and affection for my best friend didn't waver, but my ability to demonstrate it decreased as my maternal responsibilities increased. Unfortunately, this was deeply hurtful to my dear friend. Years of resentment built up over time and, ultimately, we reached a friendship impasse. Sadly, my focus on my kids' needs and all that the wrecking ball of parenthood entails kept me from meeting *her* needs—from being the kind of best friend she needed.

I am hopeful that one day, when our paths are more parallel, we can pick up where we left off. In the meantime, I find myself in a different season of friendship altogether. I have some great friends right now. Women whose houses I know I can drop my kids off for a few hours when I need a break. Friends whose kids don't revolt me and whom I'm happy to entertain for a weekend. Women with whom I can badmouth my kids' teachers and consult when I wonder if a child's rash merits a visit to urgent care at 10pm.

As a parent, friendships are perhaps the only thing keeping us sane. I crave my time with my friends, even if it's just a quick hello in the school pickup line or during an intense barre session. And while these friendships don't have the history of those I share with childhood friends, they have something that is even more powerful: empathy.

I believe that empathy is the key to healthy and thriving friendships, and no one knows empathy more than a mother. I think we all can say, "Been there, done that." And that sense of knowing—that understanding of what it is like to be in your shoes—can help us overcome even the hardest moments, like the loss of a dear, old friendship.

So, sit back and enjoy this beautiful and varied collection of essays from some of my all-time favorite bloggers. If they make you feel grateful for special friends of yours, tell them so. Even more so, act like it. Because life without them just wouldn't be the same.

Jill Smokler is the New York Times bestselling author of Confessions of A Scary Mommy *(April 2012) and* Motherhood Comes Naturally (And Other Vicious Lies) *(April 2013) as well as the owner all things Scary Mommy. Jill's website averages over 6 million page views a month, and her Twitter feed and Facebook page entertain over 435,000 people daily. Her children remain highly unimpressed.*

Introduction

In February 2013, two relatively new bloggers managed to bump into each other in a Facebook group. Recognizing common interests, shared favorite authors, and a kinship in spite of stylistic differences, they reached out to one another through blog comments, Facebook posts, and eventually email. An idea was born.

Neither of us had any idea when we first exchanged enthusiastic comments about our similar taste in books that we would be publishing one together less than one year later. The process of compiling this ensemble of essays has been illuminating and inspiring; we have both felt so privileged to bear witness to the friendship stories that have been shared. We hope these essays resonate with you as they did with both of us, and perhaps they will even move you to reflect on your own unique history of friendship.

At the beginning of this book, you will find two chapters devoted to understanding friendship. Friendship experts Shasta Nelson and Carlin Flora help to illumine the nature of female friendship and why it is so significant in women's lives.

Because so many women associate specific times of their life with different friendships, we have organized the book into four sections. In "What's New," we explore adult friendships — in real life and online. Our contributors explore the impact of technology, divorce, race, aging, and the workplace on friendships. In "What's Old," you will read stories about childhood friendships, as well as the relationships between sisters, mothers, and daughters. The "What's Changed" section is devoted to stories about friendship and motherhood. Our final section of the book,

"What's Lost," includes stories of grief, loss, and friendship breakups. Whether you identify with the new mother who struggles with loneliness, the woman who looks forward to her social media notifications, the challenging and complex relationship of sisters, or the stories of friends who have drifted apart, we believe you will recognize yourself somewhere in the pages of this book.

Each essay shines a light on a different aspect of friendship. For example, Julie Burton and Kate Hall write about their relationships with their sisters; Dana Hemelt and Rose Townsend mourn the loss of dear friends; Kristi Campbell and Samantha Brinn Merel share their vulnerable stories of friendships that have drifted apart; Christine Woodruff and Lindsey Mead reflect on the women who helped them through their transition to motherhood.

Compiling this book — and building a new working friendship — has given us both a renewed appreciation of the importance of women's friendship, which can be just as intimate as marriage and essential to emotional health. We hope you enjoy exploring this book. We think female friendship is such a rich and complex subject. The essays you are about to read reflect the multiple layers of women's friendship — the joy, the pain, and the power.

Jessica & Stephanie

Understanding Friendship

The Power of "Friendfluence"

CARLIN FLORA

You've probably spent a lot of time thinking about how your genes and your parents' actions conspired to make you who you are today. If you've been in at least one serious romantic relationship, you've probably passed a significant amount of time analyzing how *that* bond changed you as well. But what about your friends? Sure, we talk about friendship when we're grappling with a specific conflict or quandary, but we rarely ponder just how much our friends shape us, from the pre-school playground to the nursing home rec room.

I define "friendfluence" as the powerful and often unappreciated role that friends—past and present—play in determining our sense of self and the direction of our lives. We cherish friendship, yet few of us are fully aware of the specific effects friends have on our personal growth and happiness.

Humans have evolved to be extremely sensitive to the norms of the social group (or tribe) to which we belong, simply because group living and cooperation are what have enabled us to survive. When a teenager says she'll die if she doesn't get invited to so-and-so's party, she is tapping into a primal fear of social exclusion. Rejection even activates the same part of the brain that lights up when we're physically hurt.

Children are wired to find a comfortable niche in their peer group. One fact that illuminates how peers can mold children more than parents is accent acquisition. Does the daughter of immigrants speak with her parents' accent? Never. She always adopts the regional accent of her friends. Teens, of course, are deeply concerned with social dynamics and are susceptible to peer pressure, but, guess what? So are adults! We rarely admit it, but everything from our supposedly unique sense of style (friends dress like their friends) to our weight to our moods to the likelihood of our divorcing, enjoying work, or even dying at any given time is significantly influenced by our friends.

Because we conform to the habits and values of our friends, choosing yours consciously can have a big impact on your success and well-being. Get in with the wrong clique, and you could find yourself drifting away from your core ideals and beliefs. Still, nothing is worse for your mental or physical health than a total lack of friends: loneliness triggers damaging thought patterns and is linked to depression, cardiovascular disease, and alcohol and drug abuse.

If you're juggling work and family obligations, making new friends and investing in your long-term friendships understandably get bumped to the bottom of the priority list. Squeeze in time for your friends, though, and you'll be physically energized, intellectually stimulated, emotionally supported, and in better all-around shape to tackle the other areas of your life.

People are marrying later—if at all—and living alone more than ever, meaning that friends are increasingly taking on roles that used to be fulfilled by family members. All the more reason it's time to give friendship its due: Form new friendships with people you admire and who understand what you're going through right now, nurture friendships with people who have known you for a long time and really understand your patterns and personality, and go out of your way to give to your friends. Being a great friend to others is both a privilege and one of life's most rewarding pleasures.

Carlin Flora is the author of Friendfluence: The Surprising Ways Friends Make Us Who We Are. *A former editor at* Psychology Today *magazine, she has written for* Discover, Scientific American, Glamour, Women's Health, *and* Time.com, *among other publications. She has also appeared as a guest expert on* The Today Show, The Oprah Winfrey Show, 20/20 *and* Fox and Friends.

Frientimacy

SHASTA NELSON

We replace half of our close friends every seven years. Sound impossible? Think about who you would invite to stand up with you as a bridesmaid right now if you were getting married. Name five to seven potential candidates, and chances are high that at least two or three of them wouldn't have been the same ones you'd have invited if you'd gotten married seven years prior. And chances are just as high that seven years from now, two or three of them might be women you haven't even yet grown close to, or possibly even yet met. Our friendships ebb and flow.

You'll see these truths play out in this book. Its organization suggests our awareness that not all friendships are for life. Through four themes (childhood friendships, motherhood and friendship, friendship breakups/losses, and adult friendships) you'll see friendship life stages play out in broad strokes. But even within each separate story you'll read about the increasing and decreasing of Frientimacy at play. ("Frientimacy" is a word I coined to capture the non-romantic intimacy we strive to experience in our friendships.)

Recognizing that we have different categories of friends is not to minimize the uniqueness that each one brings. Rather, it helps us both to honor how we're energized in different relationships and to identify the sources of our hunger for more connectedness.

Increasing **Frientimacy with the 5 Circles of Connectedness**

I created the 5 Circles of Connectedness as a visual tool for helping us see the movement of our friendships from those circles on the Left-Side to those circles on the Right-Side, from Contact Friends to Commitment Friends. From the most casual of our friendships that depend upon a specific context for us to be connecting (i.e. work, association meetings, children's school) to the most intimate of friendship in which we confide in a friend regularly, we can trace steps along the way.

To be clear, all friendships start at Contact Friends. We never meet someone and put them in any other circle, no matter how much chemistry there is, how much we like them, or how many things we have in common with them. All friendships start on the left when they are new and then move to the right as we put into place the repeated positive behaviors that will become our friendship with that person.

We all tend to find some circles come to us more naturally. Some of us love socializing and meeting tons of Contact Friends but have a harder time building enough consistency with a few to move into the real intimacy of Commitment Friends, whereas others of us have a few close friends but hate going out and meeting people. But we all need people in every circle.

I find that many women long for more Committed Friends when they find themselves wishing for more connection in their lives. For them, it's not just knowing more people that appeals to them, but actually experiencing Frientimacy (the intimacy between safe and known friends) with a few of them that matters most. Seeing where their current friendships fall on this continuum helps them assess which friendships could be moved to the right (from other Circles) to the far right where they want them, with an intentional increase in consistency, interaction, and revealing.

The two most important actions anyone can take for increasing the bonds within a relationship is making sure the time together is consistent, meaning as frequent as possible (which might mean then that the most important action you can take is initiating that time together!), and the second is to appropriately increase the intimacy by sharing additional parts of your lives with each other. For example, someone moves from Common Friends to Community Friends simply by starting to connect with each other in a new context which might mean movie night with a work friend that you typically only see at work or going out sans kids with a woman who you only know through mom's groups or PTA meetings.

Only as we get to know each other more (in new areas and in deeper ways), which comes with time together, will we move friendships to the right.

Decreasing Frientimacy with the 5 Circles of Connectedness

As friendships grow, they move from left to right; and the converse is just as true, as friendships wane, they can move from right to left.

This is significant to us because it gives us more options than just ending friendships! We can decrease vulnerability, time together, and ways of interacting to move friendships from more intimate to less intimate.

For example, women will often say to me a variation of "I'm going through a break-up right now... my friend is x (fill in the blank with any number of circumstances that aren't some obvious friendship failings but are, nonetheless, exhausting the woman who has long called her a friend: having an affair, obsessed with losing weight, going through a divorce, dating some guy she thinks is horrible to her, or letting her entire life be run by her kids) and I can't take it anymore so, unfortunately, it's over."

But with the above Circles of Connectedness, we can mentally say, "X makes it hard to be close right now. With the amount of time we're spending together (or the limited amount of time I want to spend together right now), it's important for me to no longer see this friendship as a sustaining, meaningful, and supportive Community or Committed Friend right now so that I have appropriate expectations and boundaries with her. With the decrease in time and pulling back of confiding in her right now– she's probably more accurately in X Circle."

Moving someone to the left does two important things for us:

1. First, it helps us acknowledge that something has shifted and the friendship isn't going to be as close and safe as it has been. That means

I don't need to feel guilty for not giving as much and I can definitely be more gracious to her as I won't be expecting as much. It means that we don't have to refuse to ever see her again, but neither do we need to pour energy into staying in touch with her as much as we have previously. Now, just getting together once a month during this time is fine.

2. And second, it helps us recognize that we need to make sure we have the close and safe friends in our lives that we need for right now. It's not *her* fault for not being everything we wanted her to be as much as it is *our* responsibility to make sure we have the friends we need in our lives. So if she left a vacancy when we moved her left, then we need to look for other friendships to nurture. We need to start investing that extra time and energy into other friends.

There are many reasons to keep these women in our lives. Just because she's married now and we need some single friends doesn't mean we can't still find other things in common. Just because she tends to squirm when the conversation gets too personal doesn't mean she isn't still a fabulous and thought-provoking museum date. Just because she can get insecure and jealous doesn't mean she's not a super fun addition to your mom's night out group. Just because she doesn't have as much time now that she's a mom doesn't mean she won't be the first one we'll want to call someday when we get to that stage! And just because she's not the person who responds without judgment to your secrets doesn't mean she can't keep you inspired as a fellow artist.

In short, we can move the relationship back to where we're not over-sharing with someone we don't trust or spending too much time with someone who exhausts us, without having to let go of parts of them we do enjoy.

Our friendships don't have to be all-or-nothing. This isn't "find one to be all to us" as much as "find several who can each meet different needs of ours."

Relationships ebb and flow, wane and wax, drift and shift.

You are holding in your hands a labor of love. Certainly it's a labor of love between two friends, Jessica and Stephanie, as they committed to the gathering and telling of women's friendships stories. But it's also a labor of love from all the women who bared their hearts and revealed their truths as they showed up in relationships, practicing love with someone else. This isn't fiction. These are real women, real feelings, real elation, and real disappointment. And we invite it to be your labor of love, too. Pages that remind you of your own stories, your own friendships, and the desire for connection you will continue to labor after....

For here's the secret: it's not in spite of the labor that we love, but within that we learn what true love is. May your labors lead you to wider and deeper friendship love in your life.

Shasta Nelson, M.Div., is the Founder of GirlFriendCircles.com, *a women's friendship matching site in 35 cities across the U.S. and Canada. Her spirited and soulful voice for strong female relationships can be found in her book* Friendships Don't Just Happen! The Guide to Creating a Meaningful Circle of GirlFriends. *She also writes at* ShastasFriendshipBlog.com *and in the* Huffington Post, *speaks across the country, and is a friendship expert in the media appearing on such shows as* Katie Couric *and the* Today Show.

What's New: Grown-up Friendships, In Real Life and Online

Five Letters

GALIT BREEN

I tiptoe onto the porch. Sun slices morning sky. It's welcome.

I settle within cool air, hot coffee, and still silence.

The wooden, slatted floor is rough and cold beneath my bare feet. A bird sings her good mornings. A cyclist speeds by.

And I sit. My laptop is by my side, unopened. My unfinished work can wait.

Instead, I reach for a thin plastic bag filled with scrapbooking paper I (sadly) haven't looked at for years. But that this morning, I cut it to size, to fit a new story I'd like to tell.

I run my fingertips over greens, purples, and oranges in muted tones. I note how soft the paper is – delicate even – and my own nails' lack of shine, and need of polish. This, too, can wait.

I click open my pen and begin to write. It feels good to free my thoughts in this way. By ink, slowly, purposefully.

I'm writing a letter to a friend, one of five I'll write this month.

By heart, I know that gifting myself the time and effort of friendship is key to my balance, my happiness, and my peace.

But by mind, it's sometimes hard to pull myself away from my work and my family and my ways. There are so many things that need to be shined in my home.

Several years ago, I made the conscious decision to friend-focus in the way I tell my children to. I texted and invited and made cookies. I complimented and emailed and recommended books. I changed the way I viewed my friendships, looking for their goodness, zooming in on their light.

But I've been ignoring a small gem. Its shine is important, so I'm stepping into it now.

I've been missing the chance to tell my friends how I see them. Their goodness and their light, the way they make me feel, that they're noticed.

So this month, I'm trying something new. I'm writing letters to five women whose friendship lifts me. I'm ridiculously lucky in that when I was deciding who to write to this month, my list of choices was long, and inspiring.

So in the still of this morning – as the sun lights and my family sleeps and my neighbors run – I'm focusing out, in order to focus in.

I leave myself (mostly) out of the letters, not writing about my thoughts or my memories or my details.

Instead, I write what I see in them. The light they offer; the gifts they give.

I pen who they are through my eyes.

Your laugh fills the space between earth and sky.

You hand out second chances, without second thoughts.

People's shoulders relax around you.

Oh, how you make people laugh until their cheeks and their lips and their stomachs hurt in appreciation.

You listen in the way that makes people feel heard.

We all deserve to be seen in our most flattering lights. We also all deserve the chance to notice others in this well lit way.

Previously published at Everyday Family.

Galit Breen is a Minnesota writer. On any given day she can be found juggling three kids, one husband, one puggle, and her laptop. Galit is a women's fiction novelist, has had essays published in several anthologies, is a contributing writer to Soleil Moon Frye's Moonfrye, The Huffington Post *blog, SheKnows's* allParenting, *and* EverydayFamily, *and is the editor of* Pens and Paint, *a series anthology of children's poetry and artwork. Galit blogs at* These Little Waves *and may or may not work for dark chocolate.*

The More The Merrier

Elizabeth Suarez Aguerre

I've been thinking a lot about friendships lately.

My dearest friend's seven-year-old granddaughter is having some issues on the playground. She can't quite understand how her best friend can be her best friend one day and completely ignore her the next.

"That's just rude, Gram. *And* it hurts my feelings."

It's tough being a girl. Women are difficult creatures. We desperately need each other but we push each other away, claw and snap and bitch, and talk behind each other's backs.

My friend assured her granddaughter that "one day" she'd find that one true best friend.

"Really, Gram? You promise?"

"I promise."

I told my friend that I thought that had been a terrible promise to make (we're honest like that). I'm not sure I really believe in the notion of a best friend anymore, although lately (and here's the truly ironic part) I feel I am in some of the healthiest relationships of my life. The notion of That One True Best Friend — the promise that little girl is holding out for — puts a whole lot of pressure on her and especially on the girls around her. No *one* person should be responsible for being every *thing* to anyone.

That little girl may be so busy looking for that One Girl that she may miss out on all the ones skipping happily around her on the playground.

* * *

In spite of the fact that most people would probably describe me as very outgoing, I've actually spent most of my life being somewhat antisocial. Growing up, I was never accepted into any of the Cliques Of The Moment, and more often than not, I'd find somebody who was "like me" (read: a little too loud or a little too dramatic or a little too awkward or a little too whatever I happened to be at the time) and I'd latch on. I'd found her: my friendship soulmate! And eventually, as is almost always inevitable with females, she'd screw me over.

There was Marilyn in 3rd grade, who one day came back from lunch and abruptly and silently pulled her desk a few inches away from mine and refused to speak to me. I remember Lena, in middle school, who decided hanging out with "the other girls" was way cooler than hanging out with me (she was probably right). The list goes on and on. I realize there were probably many times that I, too, had disappointed them…I don't doubt that I said something completely inappropriate to Marilyn that day at lunch, but couldn't she have told me what that something was?

What I've come to realize over the last couple of years is that all that time I spent excluding everyone else in order to be with my One True Best Friend, I had missed out. A lot. On people, outings, experiences, adventures, life lessons.

I now find myself surrounded by a lot of really remarkable women…some I had pushed aside for years because I simply "didn't have the time" to spend with them. I am more open, less judgmental, and having a whole heck of a lot more fun. My "collection" of girlfriends are all incredibly different: with some I can discuss, in great detail, Marc Jacobs's personal make-over…others shop "exclusively" at Walmart and Target. For some of my friends, sweating is restricted to dancing and sex…others are game for anything from a 5k to a full-out adventure race. I would not call any one of these women my Best Friend. I know who I can call in the middle of the night when my kid is running a fever of 105. I know who I can call when I'm desperate for a night of dancing and drinks. Some of these women know secrets about me that the rest of the world would be shocked to know. Others, I'm just starting to truly trust.

Today, I "asked a girl out." Well, that's what it felt like, anyway.

I recently started to talk to someone at work who seems to be so amazingly interesting and intelligent and just plain "cool," that I stepped out of my old comfort zone and, after 30 minutes of chatting about designer galoshes, world-wide travel, Christian Louboutins, mamas' boys, marriage and children, I decided to make a plan to get together next week. This may seem like a totally normal thing to do. But for me, it felt foreign.

This woman may become one of my girls. Or, perhaps we will get together and have absolutely nothing to talk about (although after that 30-minute-all-inclusive-chat, I doubt it!). But the point is that I have finally figured out that I don't need one Best Friend. I need lots of really fantastic friends. I am no longer disappointed, because I don't put all my eggs in one basket. I have lots of baskets, and I'm skipping happily around with them on the playground.

Elizabeth Suarez Aguerre is a teacher, writer, blogger, mommy, wife, and beach bum. She is the published author of 9 educational books, and bluntly expresses her very passionate opinions on her blog, But Then I Had Kids, *which she started in 2009 in an attempt to survive the early days of new motherhood.*

The Wired Momma Guide to Making Friends as an Adult

MONICA SAKALA

"Kindred spirits are not so scarce as I used to think. It's splendid to find out there are so many of them in the world." – L.M. Montgomery, Anne of Green Gables

That phrase, kindred spirits, grabbed me at such a young age, when I was deeply in love with Anne of Green Gables (and Gilbert Blythe, obviously). I knew from that moment that I would always need kindred spirits in my life. Having been a child of a Foreign Service officer, I knew from spending my childhood moving every three years that kindred spirits stay with you, no matter the distance between you.What I never considered until I grew up and had kids of my own, however, was that finding kindred spirits of my own would become infinitely harder — or, rather, I would have to be more creative in looking for them. At times, without some creative thinking, kindred spirits could feel utterly scarce. And no one needs a kindred spirit more than when she's just had a baby.

This fact rang even more true in the summer of 2012 when Alex Williams published a piece in the Sunday *New York Times* titled "Making Friends at a Certain Age." Williams did a brilliant job of breaking down the reality of the difficulty in finding new friends as we age.

In his article, Williams notes that life becomes more complicated as we age and also, frankly, we have much less tolerance for something we might consider cute or funny or quirky about someone when we are older. Enter a tired, cranky, short on patience 30-something with a few demanding toddlers and a quirky adult who is flaky or constantly late (both of these characteristics describe me, by the way) — and forget it — friendship ain't gonna happen.

Also, we all have serious time constraints. Williams lays out the conditions "crucial to making close friends: proximity; repeated, unplanned interactions; and a setting that encourages people to let their guard down and confide in each other."

So what circumstances led me to find my adult kindred spirits? For me, it was my backyard fence and my preschool.

Let's start with the fence. Where else, as busy adults, can you find proximity, repeated unplanned interactions and a place to let your guard down than your fence in the back yard? This space can encompass more than your backyard; it can include your entire neighborhood. Truth be told, there were many times I roved the streets of my neighborhood, like a brave explorer, on a quest to discover the only survival tool for the parent in the late afternoon: impromptu happy hour. In this realm of extreme parenting, I am a true Olympian. Read: I was usually successful — perhaps I can smell wine 5 miles away? In fact, my mantle is now laden with gold medals.

I'm not sure how you hone in on the right neighborhood when you are moving to a new city but we lucked out. Having spent my entire childhood moving every few years to a new country, I never really knew what having a neighbor meant, let alone putting down roots in a neighborhood. Sometimes I wondered about it — but not really — I was a kid and I had what I needed. Now, I know. Having a next door neighbor or great neighborhood friends meets the criteria of proximity and unplanned interactions. I spent eight years at that backyard fence with my next door neighbor, Julie, and it was never planned. She was standing in the driveway when we pulled up with our first-born for the first time (and I was crying and terrified) and her boys being older than my girls provided endless blog fodder and insight for me into what was coming my way. Over eight years, everyone moves through some pretty major milestones, whether it be marriage, divorce, pregnancies, loss and certainly in Montgomery County, chronic power outages. So if you're on the hunt for a great friend but you're short on time, look next door or on your street.

I think neighborhood listservs have been one of the most helpful ways to foster relationships. The key is being willing to put yourself out there. Crash a few yards, or be out front with a glass of wine around 5 p.m., and you'll be surprised what comes your way (There are Olympian happy hour crashers in every neighborhood. Of this, I am certain). People will stop, they will pull their cars over – make shift happy hours can make for great friendships. Trust moi.

The second part of finding new friends for me has been preschool. Again, this was unplanned. I went into it not even considering the new adults around me or how I might someday be vacationing with them. Instead, I was solely focused on getting our oldest into preschool. I lucked out. Again. What I've since decided is preschool is preschool — what do they do but play? Well, they learn to raise their hand and share, kind of, but other than that, they play. And trade in nasty illnesses with disturbing names (Hand, Foot & Mouth, anyone?). Don't kid yourself otherwise. So when picking out preschool for your child, in retrospect, the best advice is to pick a school that attracts the kind of parents you want to be *friends with*. Sure, you're not going to like all the parents. But the philosophy and approach of the school is about more than just how they educate your child all day long; it's also about your outlook on parenting and life. So here's where you want to find other kindred spirits.

The sister wives from preschool are my people. Along with my early 20s-working-people, my grad school people and my neighborhood people. But the sister wives from preschool are the people I least expected to have in my life, because I wasn't looking for them, didn't know I needed them, and didn't know I was missing them.

You need sister wives from preschool because your kids are the same age and as the kids get older (and the lovely moms remarkably never age), your chances of them playing together increases, so you can have uninterrupted conversations. It does happen.

What about if you are in that lonely place of having a newborn or a baby but you aren't yet to preschool or you've moved or both have happened? How do you find these new friends? The new people who can relate to your life as it is now, not how it was before you had a husband and children? Unfortunately, I don't know the answer but everyone needs people. Again, I think putting yourself out there is key — literally asking people to be friends. I have met many women at random music classes or parks who have told me how they've almost accosted other women, basically asking them to be friends. I also defer back to neighborhood listservs and putting yourself out there — asking for a play date. And the accidental casual glass of wine out front during the early evening. Don't forget that one. You'll need the kids out front too, otherwise you could look kind of pathetic and desperate.

The park is also prime friend-meeting territory. But tread lightly. Odds are the person next to you at the swings is also equally as bored with pushing their kid by about the 35th push. But read their body language like you do the seat mate on the airplane. They are either exuding friendliness or they don't want you to talk to them and wish they had a book to stick their nose in, even if they, too, are bored. If they appear friendly, then before you know it, happy hour could be scheduled, disguised as a play date.

And in the end, I think as adults, it's not about quantity but quality. All those people on Facebook pages, Twitter feeds and from college parties aren't necessarily real friends – I think most of us just need a small few key people.

Everyone needs a fence, a neighbor, and some sister wives. Everyone needs kindred spirits.

"We'll be Friends Forever, won't we, Pooh?' asked Piglet.
Even longer,' Pooh answered."
– A.A. Milne, Winnie-the-Pooh

After a dozen years working in public affairs in Washington DC, Monica Sakala stepped away in 2008 to stay home with her two young daughters. One day she realized it's possible she suffers from Stockholm Syndrome and turned to Google to confirm life with a toddler is, in fact, a form of torture under the Geneva Convention. She found the only way to escape the brutal reality of living under a toddler regime was a blog, and so Wired Momma *was born. Monica also runs her own consulting company, SOMA Strategies, helping clients develop social media campaigns.*

Friends and Divorce

SHANNAN BALL YOUNGER

"You'll find out who your true friends are."

Someone told me that when I was at the very beginning of my divorce, and they were right. But that wasn't the whole story. I learned so much more than just the identity of who my true friends were.

I learned that I have a lot more friends than I ever realized.

It's easy to feel lonely during a difficult time, especially a divorce, but my friends made that difficult. That was particularly shocking to me because I had not been a good friend to many as my marriage disintegrated. I don't think that I had much left to give to anyone by the time it was finally over.

And much to my chagrin, that was okay.

These people who deserved so much better from me were continuing to gift me with their friendship. Each in his/her own way let me know that they had my back, be it by sending flowers on my birthday just a few days after I had moved into my new apartment or notes or leaving cheery voicemail messages.

There were many gestures full of love and, at a time when I felt unlovable, it was overwhelming.

Side note: I learned that my friends are big Elizabeth Gilbert fans as many, many copies of *Eat, Pray, Love* flooded into my new apartment. It made me laugh. I didn't know what to do with so many copies of the same book, but as other friends entered the process of divorce, they eventually found homes. I wonder if those friends also got multiple copies and were too kind to tell me. (And I trust that my friends are okay with me regifting.)

I learned that I underestimate my friends.

There was one friend in particular who is a very staunch, devout Catholic. Her faith is supremely significant to her. I thought she would have a hard time with my divorce, especially since it was something that I initiated. I worried that we would not remain friendly because I wasn't sure she'd be able to look past my decision to kick a sacrament to the curb. I was wrong. Very, very wrong.

The friend that I had thought I was likely to lose, who I was fully prepared to count among the casualties of my decision, was amazing. She supported me and loved me. Years later, she's the one who will call on a holiday when I don't have my daughter to see how I am doing. Of all my friends, she is one who really gets it. And gets me.

I am ashamed because I completely underestimated her. Strange as it is, I think my divorce may have even brought us closer. I saw her in a new light, and I wondered what else I had misjudged about her.

I also wondered how much underestimating I had done with many of my friends. How unfair had I been? How much had I let myself paint a picture of our relationship for them rather than just letting the image unfold on its own?

I lost a few friends in the process, of course. We had joint friends, and some aligned with him, as is to be expected.

What I did not expect to learn, though, was that I had failed to appreciate the wonderfulness of the friends who stuck around and I've made a conscious effort to not underestimate them moving forward.

Shannan Ball Younger hangs out in the suburbs of Chicago with her husband and tween daughter. She blogs about parenting and weathering the hormone hurricane that comes with a tween at Tween Us. *She also blogs at* Families in the Loop *and* Chicago Parent *and was part of the* Listen to Your Mother: Chicago 2013 *cast. A recovering attorney who works at a small nonprofit, she was excited to be quoted by the BBC, but hoping that they come back again soon to talk about something other than Justin Bieber.*

Leslie and Me

Carisa Miller

- She has chosen not to have children.
- I, eyebrow deep in tiny pink clothes, am mother to two daughters.

My children have loved Leslie from birth. They leap forward into her arms as though she is also their most intimate friend. It is remarkable, especially since they see her only briefly every few months. They must sense my love for her and her love for them.

- She does not drink alcohol.
- I enjoy the bounty of fermented fruits from our glorious local wine and beer economy.

Far from the days of mass consumption and hangovers, I prefer to keep my faculties sharp. I need to preserve my remaining brainpower since my supply was greatly diminished by the onset of offspring. Contrariwise, sometimes by the end of the day my brain requires a Pinot Noir rinse.

- She does not shave.
- I have succumbed to the odd societal standard that pre-pubescent-esque hairlessness is sexy.

She attended my wedding in a flowing sleeveless dress. My father elbow-jabbed his cousin to point out the girl who was "smuggling gophers under her arms." Leslie loves that joke.

- **She is the official spokeswoman for a well-contemplated life.**
- **I've still got some catching up to do.**

Time spent with Leslie is likely to include discussing the downfalls of mono-crop agriculture, the movement to rebuild a healthy local ecology, and the state of our personal lives in regard to our lifetime goals and ideals. The woman runs deep.

- **Her style is timeless.**
- **Mine is attempting timeless, but generally runs in more of a covered-in-boogers direction.**

Prior to children, I enjoyed the hunt for new clothes. Now my apparel shopping consists mainly of me lying in wait to steal whatever Leslie is wearing when she comes for a visit. I'm not kidding. One time she barely got through the door before I had nearly talked her out of her new purse.

- **She is a gardening dynamo, has a vast knowledge of botanical Latin, and is a certified Master Gardener.**
- **I fake it. Sure, I've learned quite a bit over the years, but I still usually just drag whatever plant I want to whichever spot I want it, throw it in a hole and cross my fingers.**

Gardening is a way of life I didn't know before Leslie. She inspired my now insatiable lust for ornamentals and taught me the great value of self-grown edibles.

- **She eats the bejeezus out of leafy greens.**
- **She never ceases to be amused by my ability to subsist primarily on cheese.**

Beginning with Leslie, I've come to understand the value, deliciousness and responsibility of eating organic and local food...covered in cheese.

- **She is of the Baha'i faith.**
- **I believe in a my own personal blend of Natural Pantheism, Moon Worship, Paganism, Buddhism and Atheism.**

One year, I participated with Leslie in the Baha'i month of fasting.

For nineteen days we did not eat or drink between sunrise and sunset. She appreciated my support. I appreciated the sunset.

- **She plays the cello.**
- **I'm all about ballet. However, in high school I was accidentally a cheerleader.**

Oops.

- **When she was single, she was not the least affected by a desire not to be.**
- **I was so eager to be in a relationship, I frantically scrambled around trying to grab at and squeeze love from a bunch of jerks.**

Leslie tirelessly repeated how deserving I was of a healthy relationship and pointed out all evidence indicating I was heading in the wrong direction. Instead of giving me up for lost each time I cycled round through the same old drama, she showed up on my doorstep with flowers, ready to listen to me cry. Once I joined her in believing that I was a worthy woman, she taught me how to spot a decent man and I eventually got it right. <enter husband of my dreams>

- **She is engaging. She truly listens.**

- I struggle to find questions to ask people about themselves. Though I strive to be a good listener, it doesn't come naturally to me.

Leslie cares to know about people. She hears what they say and asks follow-up questions. I greatly admire her caring and considerate nature. I tend to be too absorbed in my own thoughts to be very engaging.

- She knows where everything goes.
- I cannot hang a piece of art, arrange flowers or furniture without trying to see it through her eyes in order to get it right.

Meaningful living and aesthetic design may not, at first, appear to have much in common. But Leslie and I understand the pleasing beauty of a perfectly arranged bookshelf can be as enriching as the contents of the books contained within. She turned me on to the elements of design. We spend a lot of our time together waving our arms around and discussing use of space.

- She is blunt and honest, with no frilly facade.
- I am that way too, with Leslie and a few select people. With most others I am easily nervous and tend to blurt nonsense instead of what I mean to say.

My relationship with Leslie contains zero fluff, tiptoeing, or sugar coated bologna. With all the time and effort we save not skirting around truths, we are able to scrape at the depths of ourselves and give attention to the guts of our lives. If she thinks I'm not seeing a situation clearly, or acting appropriately, Leslie tells me flat out. If Leslie is about to quit her job to pursue hula-hooping full time, I'm the first to call her crazy. (I made that up. The job part, not the hoop. She's pretty good.)

- She lets herself be known.
- Ditto.

When I asked Leslie if I could write about her, she was all for it. When I asked if there was anything off-limits she told me she preferred to live out in the open. Well put. I am all for this.

- **She lives by her beliefs.**
- **I am spoiled by comfort.**

No matter whether I think it is a great idea to stop sending all that water down the pipes, I'm not disconnecting the drains from the sinks in our house to collect usable gray water or switching to composting toilets any time soon (read never).

If you were keeping score while reading this you will have arrived at the conclusion that Leslie is a loving, sober, hairy, well-dressed, artistic, engaging, educated, musical, faithful, forthright, lettuce-loving, contemplative gardener living by her convictions in a house with a surprisingly delightful waterless toilet. Which makes me a baby-toting, wine-lipped, cheese-clogged, snot-covered, stubbly, nervous, babbling, loud-mouthed, water-wasting, faithless, dancing plant terrorist. Yep, that sounds about right.

Some of our differences are significant, but our shared traits and passions are far more so. The respect Leslie and I have for each other is tremendous. Everything she shares with me enriches my life, most of all herself. Leslie is a woman of unequivocal quality. I am blessed that she calls me her friend.

Carisa Miller is a sarcasm wielding, cherub lugging, cheese devouring nut job writer. She lives in Portland, Oregon with her astonishingly patient husband, two fireball daughters, and an ill- tempered cat. Her haphazard adventures in baby raising, gardening, crafting, cooking and everything else are strewn across her website, Carisa Miller: Do You Read Me?, *where serious undertones and actual information may occasionally appear amid one-liners and run-on sentences.*

How to Ask Ignorant Questions of a Black Person

JESSICA NULL VEALITZEK

I feel, as a lifelong student of black-white race relations–albeit a white one–that the only way to improve race relations is to talk and talk and talk and get to know.

I think we especially need to ask ignorant questions, as long as they are borne of respect and a desire to learn. Otherwise, how do we get less ignorant? If we intend to *know*, then we might hurt, we might offend, but only momentarily. Bit by bit, we'll go forward.

Below is an actual Facebook conversation I had with my friend, Melanie. I asked her questions that have peeked around my mind on several occasions.

Jessica Null Vealitzek

- First, do you prefer black or African-American? Are the (respectful) labels something black folks like you care about or are they something that certain spokespeople just make up? And, do you hate that question?

Melanie

- I think the label thing is a funny one because personally I don't care. I like African American and I like black. However, I know several people who have a definite feeling about it. A friend of

mine prefers black, others push hard to be called African
American.

- I think that's a safe question. "Safe" meaning that's about as far
as most people go when it comes to asking questions about race.

Jessica Null Vealitzek

- So either is ok for you. I'll go with black because it's shorter.
- Here goes. I would not be friends with you if you were not the
funny, supportive, and intelligent person that you are. But I
have to confess. I'm glad I have a friend who is black. I like
meeting new people, especially those who will expand my
knowledge and experiences. Does this undercut our friendship?

Melanie

- It doesn't undercut our friendship. You shouldn't feel bad about
it because I feel that you and I are friends because we're friends
and you like me as a person. It's just nice that I'm black, because
it enriches your experience, enriches your life experience.
- Though you do have to recognize that it's a privilege for you,
that you exercise, to have that feeling.

Jessica Null Vealitzek

- Will you say more?

Melanie

- Sure, you think it's neat that I'm black and that you have a black
friend, but I don't have that. Many of my friends are going to be
white and I have to explain things or brace myself for
insensitive comments.
- You can just go about your daily life and be you; me, I have a bit
of a guard up when I meet people because I've been hurt so
many times in the past.

Jessica Null Vealitzek

- Got it. Do you think that all that bracing yourself, though valid, can lead to defensiveness? How do you draw the line?

Melanie

- I think that I hope for the best and prepare for the worst.

Jessica Null Vealitzek

- How are black people and white people different in your eyes?

Melanie

- Oh there's so many ways that white people and black people are different, but neither group is monolithic. So that's a hard question and I could spend all day on it making a list and then creating caveats for that list.

Jessica Null Vealitzek

- Give just a couple colorful (no pun intended) examples.

Melanie

- OK
- One, I feel that black people are more honest in their feelings
- They are more likely to tell it like it is
- The white people that I've come across are more focused on putting up that perfect veneer, and it feels fake and forced and I don't have time for that so I really seek out the authentic people

Jessica Null Vealitzek

- I don't know that it's necessarily perfection some want to put forward. It's just a discomfort with showing a lot of emotion.
- But I see your point. Black people seem more willing to let that emotion out.

Melanie

- RACIST!

Jessica Null Vealitzek

- Cheeky.
- Can I tell you a story? I was on a plane last year and a large black family was seated all around me. As the plane takes off, they all start laughing and making joyful noises and I say to the man next to me, "Is this your first time flying?" and he says, "No, we just love it!" No white family would do that.

Melanie

- True. Ask yourself, why did you ask him that?

Jessica Null Vealitzek

- Because they were SO into it. I figured, this must be their first time.

Melanie

- But still, would I think they were "so" into it or just having a good time? See what I mean?
- You should see my family ride the Metro. We howl because, well, we're funny and we're cracking jokes. We're crazy and enjoy each other.

Jessica Null Vealitzek

- Yes – I think white people (the ones I know) are more reserved, so even if we thought it was fun, we wouldn't be so open about it–unless everyone else was open about it.
- Or unless we were drunk.

Melanie

- Just curious, if that was a boisterious white family would you think, *hmmm first time*?

Jessica Null Vealitzek

- I think I would, yes.

Melanie

- Maybe so, maybe not, but it's important to probe ourselves (ouch).

Jessica Null Vealitzek

- Yuck.

Melanie

- And ask ourselves those questions because we find out more about ourselves and where we sit with things.

Jessica Null Vealitzek

- Yes – exactly. And that's part of why that story has stuck with me. Also, because I just love and am jealous of being able to find that much joy in something you've done, as he said, "a million times." And being able to express it so openly.

Melanie

- [Responding to my earlier comment about needing to be drunk to be expressive] Yes and I don't like drunk white people. That's when the inhibitions drop and the comments can easily start flying.
- Do you remember when we went to that Cubs game and on the bus ride home this guy just randomly tells me that he thinks black people are cool?
- That sucked. It was like a hush fell over the bus and I was so embarrassed.

Jessica Null Vealitzek

- Yes – I think he wouldn't have said that if he wasn't drunk, but it came from a real place in him that is worried about being racist and not wanting to be.

- I think we white people can be self-conscious about all our thoughts because we worry something we think or do or say is racist.

Melanie

- I think there's grades of racism. I think that everyone's afraid of being a "big bad racist" and so they back away from conversations or avoid probing their own thoughts, for fear of what they'll find.
- We all have "isms" and judgments that we make, if we want to grow as people we need to address these issues, have honest conversations.

Jessica Null Vealitzek

- Yes. Few people consider themselves racist, but there are many grades, as you say.

Melanie

- I always say if you wouldn't say something like that to a white person then don't say it to a black person.

Jessica Null Vealitzek

- Good point.

Melanie

- But even just out of the blue pointing that out, hurts.
- Just feeling that he needed to say that, make a statement "YOU KNOW I LIKE BLACK PEOPLE." Well, OK, why wouldn't you like black people? Why do you feel the need to say that? What are you really thinking?
- Here I am having a good time, then out of left field someone is clearly seeing my color, but they're telling me they're OK with it.

- It had the same effect on me as if he would have said, "You know, I really don't like black people."

Jessica Null Vealitzek

- That is such an important point.

Melanie

- To show you how much that kind of stuff hurts, after I got home, I cried. I cried and cried because it's like damn. I let my guard down and then out of left field here this comes.
- I even found myself thinking that I should have known something like that could happen, especially since I was at a Cubs game.

Jessica Null Vealitzek

- Huh, unfortunately true.
- Back to an earlier question, Do you act differently with your friends who are white?

Melanie

- I do act a little differently. I think with my black friends I'm more relaxed, more open.
- With my white ones I'm more reserved because I don't want to feel like I'm the "entertainer."
- I also, though, don't know if it's because my black friends that I have here I've known longer than many of my white friends.
- Of course there's some white friends I've had since elementary school, and I'm 100% myself with them.

Jessica Null Vealitzek

- As someone with an interest in American history, especially the Civil War, I've always wanted to ask you about your family history. Were your ancestors slaves?

Melanie

- Yes, we were owned by the Nulls.
- Actually, we're pretty lucky to be able to trace our family history back to slavery because since a lot of us couldn't read or write, as it was against the law, a lot of the history is lost. Also because people don't want to pass on the oral histories.

Jessica Null Vealitzek

- Can you say more?

Melanie

- The previous generations didn't always want to talk about our history. There's often a shame that comes with being a slave. It's just like how people feel ashamed when they are marginalized, abused, raped. All of that and more happened to us, so many from generations ago didn't want to talk about it, didn't want to relive it.
- That's pervasive even today. I remember my grandmother mentioned to me that her and my grandfather would drive dozens of miles out of the way to visit a church because the direct route would take them through a town where "they lynched that poor man." I began asking her questions and she changed the subject as well as gave me a stern look that told me: Don't ask.
- But on my mom's side they came from a plantation in Kentucky, I believe.
- On my dad's mother's side we are related to Frederick Douglas and fought alongside the abolitionists. We have a knife in our family that John Brown gave to my relative for protection. On my dad's father's side, we came north to Kansas with the exodusters.

Jessica Null Vealitzek

- Wow. I am so asking you more about this later.

Melanie

- Yeah, it's a rich history and I love it.

Jessica Null Vealitzek

- I actually just found out through research that my ancestors in Virginia owned slaves. We also have a guy who left Canada to join the Union Army as soon as he turned 18. So, a mixed bag.

Melanie

- I think that's what we all are. A mixed bag.
- I've got whites in my family, I'm sure you've got blacks in yours. We are a melting pot, we should just recognize and *respect* differences.

Jessica Null Vealitzek

- One more question. Does it annoy you when I say things like "Girl, you crazy." Cuz you know I always do that.

Melanie

- Again, I call it the white man rule, stemming from journalism. If you wouldn't write something about a 40-year-old white man because it sounds odd, then there's no need to do it to a black guy.
- i.e. Jason Smith, who is black, was arrested for stealing a car
- Jason Smith, who is white, was arrested for stealing...
- You get the idea.
- So if IF you were a person who said "Guuurrrlll you crazy," to anyone, then fine, but don't bust out the ebonics just for me. It's insulting
- I've been dealing with that forever. I remember in high school, I gave a speech that was basically saying, "I'm not your homie. I understand, *Hello, how are you.*"

Jessica Null Vealitzek

- That's the thing. I would say that to anyone, but I've stopped myself because I don't want you to think I'm doing it because you're black. See, it's all so complicated.

Melanie

- But I do have a girlfriend who is blond haired and blue-eyed and as hood rat as they come. (She grew up in Cleveland and spent some time in Detroit too.) So when she says it, she's just being herself. No disrespect.
- But when Jill* says that shit, I call her out on it because she wouldn't say it to her white friends.

Jessica Null Vealitzek

- Right. And I have no street cred, which is why I don't want to bust it out, but sometimes it just comes to mind, you know?

Melanie

- No—does it come to mind period or just with me?

Jessica Null Vealitzek

- It comes to mind, period. With all my friends. Different sayings, ways of speaking, etc. Things I hear. It's like anything else.
- I do have to run. Thanks so much. Love you more than my luggage!

Melanie

- Nice. So you want me to carry your luggage now.
- Yes, missus.

Jessica Null Vealitzek

- I can't get anything past you.
- It's from the whitest movie on Earth.

Melanie

- Nothing like a little slave humor to wrap this thing up.

Name changed.

Jessica Null Vealitzek was born and raised near Chicago, where she still lives with her husband and two children. Her debut novel, The Rooms Are Filled, *will be published in 2014 by She Writes Press. She can be found online at* www.JessicaVealitzek.com.

Ping! How Social Media Saved My Friendship

ALLISON CARTER

I don't keep friends well.

I am a stubborn, loyal Scorpio who hates loss and distance but I'm also not the type of person who keeps a close-knit group of friends for life. (I never was in a sorority for a reason.)

I am not sure why I have this flaw. Maybe it is because I was a military brat through elementary school. Maybe it is because I went to three different high schools and three different colleges. Maybe it is because I really, truly love meeting new people and get excited to hear new stories. Maybe it is my sense of adventure that causes me to move on too fast. Maybe it is because I hate feeling like a friend is clinging to me or too needy (I'll just let you down, I am sure). Whatever the reason — to be discovered only by means of a psychologist's couch — I never wore half of a BFF heart necklace.

I get caught up in this fact sometimes, and it brings out the ugly in me: jealousy, a little depression, and a lot of self-doubt. Why don't I have a group of five friends I sit around a coffee shop with all the time, or a gang of four friends I always meet at a small bar in NYC?

Yet inevitably when I start to get this way I immediately get a "PING" and a GChat message from the one person who can rescue me from the dark thoughts: Kathy.

Kathy and I met in elementary school. In middle school, my parents had me follow my brother and moved me to a local Catholic school to finish out seventh and eighth grade. In ninth grade I moved back in to the public high school system and I remember reconnecting with Kathy. We shared the same wild and crazy English teacher.

When I moved to a different state in tenth grade, Kathy and I kept in touch. We *wrote letters*. Gasp. We wrote long letters, sent pictures, sent cards... I have a terrible memory and honestly don't remember much — that's why I blog now, it helps me remember — so I honestly couldn't say if Kathy and I were soul sisters when we lived a few miles apart. But I do know that over the course of a pen pal relationship I confided in her things I didn't tell others. Something about the distance of paper, knowing that the words could not provoke an immediate reaction I might not want to see, made me feel safe. And Lord knows, in the teenage times everyone needs a place to feel safe.

Over the years she grew to know more about me than any one. When the digital age made it even easier to connect (remember AOL IM?) we realized that we had even more in common: celebrity snark, online shopping, and career aspirations.

Then we both had kids. We had babies relatively close in age to each other. Before pregnancy both of us confided in each other our fears, hopes, concerns, and worries. Would pregnancy change us? What about losing control of our bodies? The Fashion – Lord, the fashion! Were our husbands ready for this?

But we both jumped, holding each other's hands in a virtual way.

Then at the next fork in the road we went in drastically different directions: I decided to stay at home, she decided to stay at work. I have seen this be divisive in many friendships, creating considerable coolness between once close friends. After all, working moms and stay at home moms have different concerns, issues, and problems facing them. Neither one is more difficult than the other, they are just so, well, *different*.

Yet Kathy and I have made it. Sure, we tend to talk past each other a little at times – me frazzled and just wanting to take a shower, her frustrated that she doesn't get more support trying to do it all – but we are there for each other all the way.

I wish I could share our tips with all the mothers out there: how to keep a friendship alive through the very different choices of motherhood. But I don't know why we work. I think it has to do with our deep history. I think it has to do with our personalities. (We have an ongoing joke that

I am like her husband and she is like mine so we clearly know how to handle each other.) I also think it has to do with the fact that we have never been the sort of friends that get together all the time, vacation together, or talk on the phone. Our friendship grew out of written forms of communication and those forms keep it alive today. Accordingly, the fact that neither of us has time to talk on the phone at night changes nothing at all. It isn't a missed ritual because it was never an expectation to begin with.

Some day Kathy and I are going on a girls' trip; we always have fun when we are together. Her humorous sarcasm, honesty, and ability to put down a good margarita make me love her company all the time. But we know how to maintain our friendship until all the pregnancies, baby birthing, breast feeding, and toddler-demands are finished. Then it's Chicago Or Bust. I do know that until then I will always be hooked in to my social media platforms, waiting for that daily "PING."

Allison Carter is a freelance writer who lives in Chapel Hill, NC. She blogs at Go Dansker Mom, *but also spends a lot of her time managing a local parents' guide,* Mom in Chapel Hill. *She and her husband have a 4 year old boy and a 2 year old boy so she spends a lot of time yelling, frantically, "BAD IDEA." She wouldn't have it any other way.*

When Friendships Get Real

Kelcey Kintner

I don't have a lot of tolerance for small talk. I can do it. In fact, pretty well. I once had a 22-minute conversation about throw pillows. I really don't know anything about throw pillows.

But small talk can leave me feeling empty. I want to feel a connection. I want to know more about people.

In the last few years since we left New York City, I have met many new mom friends. Just using the term "mom friends" makes me feel like I'm in a TV commercial trying to sell you my spring fresh laundry detergent. But I'm truly grateful for these friends because I had some very lonely months when I first arrived in town.

But I often find myself longing for more depth in these relationships. What did these moms do professionally before they stood on the playground waiting for their first grader to come out of school? What do they dream about when they aren't wrestling their toddler into a down jacket? (The hat and mittens? Ugh. Not even worth the effort.) Are they happy? Did they marry the right person? Do they have a moment they wish they could live over? Are they close to their parents? I want to know their story.

I blog. So for those who read it, my life is on display. Somewhat. But most moms I meet don't have blogs — and you thought *everyone* had a blog — so how am I supposed to know them?

I realize it's not always possible to have deep, involved conversations. Kids interrupt, play dates are waiting and sometimes all we really want to do is complain about the weather and go home. But it is so nice when conversations are less superficial and you feel like you are truly getting to know someone.

I was recently talking to a mom from one of my daughter's classes and she was discussing her role as a step-mom and some of the challenges. I was fascinated. The discussion had meaning. I need more of that.

I guess this is why the death of Jeffrey Zaslow affected me so much. He was a writer and father of three daughters who wasn't even on my radar screen. But my husband sent me a link to a story about his death in a car accident and I just couldn't stop reading about this guy.

He was a well known writer, co-authoring books with the former Congresswoman and gun shot victim Gabrielle Giffords, Chesley B. Sullenberger III, the pilot who landed an airplane on the Hudson River, and professor Randy Pausch, who delivered the famous "Last Lecture" when he was dying of cancer.

Zaslow was also a columnist for the *Wall Street Journal* and was so talented at writing about people and the things that mattered. Like when his daughter's date to the homecoming dance ended up not taking her at all, Zaslow wrote about it. In the *Wall Street Journal*. Think that kid regretted not taking her to the dance?

But the article was about the importance of raising our sons well and teaching our daughters to settle for nothing less than what they deserve.

As I read through some of Zaslow's columns, I felt like I truly knew the people he was writing about. I felt like I knew him. I was so touched by his realness.

And I guess, ultimately that's what I want from my life and my friendships.

Fewer throw pillows. More realness.

Kelcey Kintner has worked in the White House, been a TV reporter and earned a journalism degree from Columbia University. But nothing has ever kicked her bum like motherhood. She is the mother of five young children and drives a gold minivan because she can't fit them all on a Vespa. She writes at The Mama Bird Diaries, *a humor parenting blog and various other places but secretly longs to be an Olympic ice skater.*

Friendships Form In the Most Unlikely of Places

Julie DeNeen

Friendships form in the most unlikely of places. You don't think your life is going to change because you've met someone new. And sometimes it doesn't.

But once in a while, it does.

It was April 2011. I was in the throes of the deepest and darkest crisis of my life. Having reunited with my birth father in early 2011, our relationship had spiraled out of control and was on the fast track towards the most dysfunctional relationship you can imagine.

We'd been separated for nearly 30 years and our reunion was the kind of event you'd see in the movies. Father and daughter reconnected after a long separation. For the first few months, life was blissful. I was back with my father and starting to imagine a whole new life and family. Unbeknownst to me, the intimacy in our reunion was slowly morphing into something very dangerous.

My father eventually pursued me sexually. And despite my shock, horror, and initial disgust, eventually I gave in. Grasping for what little I had, I wanted to do anything to secure his permanence in my life, even if that meant entertaining his sexual fantasies.

After a few traumatic episodes, I was desperate for help. No one in my life knew what I was going through – having no friends who were adopted, I felt very alone.

Turning to Google one evening, I searched online for stories like mine. "Someone somewhere has to have dealt with this madness," I thought. A few clicks later, I had stumbled on a blog.

I read every entry – gasping for breath when I realized whomever this writer was, she was going through the same thing as me. Since it was an anonymous blog, I had no idea who it was behind the words, but I knew I had to talk to her.

I hit the "contact" button and sent an email to my mystery lifeline. She responded quickly and within minutes, we were friends on Facebook, chatting in the message box.

> Me: *This is weird huh?*
> Carly: *Yep. I just knew when I read your email we should talk.*
> Me: *I can't believe there is someone else in the world going through the same thing!*
> Carly: *Let me call you.*

I'll never forget that first phone call. There were no pleasantries or exchanges about the weather. From the moment I said hello, we dove into the grimy and gritty reality of what both of us were facing – reunited birth fathers who had turned our reunions into sexual escapades.

They (whomever *they* is) say that people bond during trauma. Carly and I bonded instantly that spring, talking nearly every day. We formed a fast friendship and depended on one another when no one else could understand. Our first meeting was in the Animal Kingdom down in Disney World—July 2011, three months after we started talking.

By December of 2011, both of us had successfully extricated ourselves from these toxic relationships with our fathers. Back on solid ground, Carly suggested we start a new blog to talk about the hidden nature of complicated adoptive reunions. She closed her original website and we began a new journey together.

As these things go, the blog turned into something we couldn't have imagined. Four months later we were co-owners of an entire community of people looking for help. The blog exploded and several big press outlets contacted us.

Through the next year, Carly and I traveled to Los Angeles, interviewed with ABC news, and flew to Madrid for an adoption conference.

What started out as a horrific nightmare turned into something beautiful. An unlikely friendship that altered my life, changed my perspective, and set me on a new course.

Julie DeNeen is a full time freelance writer and blogger. She authors a popular personal blog called Julie DeNeen 2.0, *and also runs a successful blog consulting business at* Fabulousblogging.com.

Friends Are the Family We Choose for Ourselves: My Sole Sisters

Hollie Deline

My husband and I moved to Denver in late September of 2008. I had left behind a close-knit community of people in a small town in southern Utah. There were the other employees at the animal rescue organization I worked for, the people I practiced yoga and Zumba with every week at the small local gym, and the friends I used to hike, camp, and adventure with on weekends.

But the biggest void in my life was left by the group of women I used to belly dance with. It was an eclectic group, all different ages, body shapes and sizes. The joy of dancing and performing with this group was something that I missed deeply.

I was able keep my job and work remotely from Denver, but I found the long days alone in my home office very lonely. I missed the boisterous office environment back at the sanctuary, complete with office dogs and cats and lots of like-minded people collaborating daily to rescue at-risk animals and improve their quality of life and chances for adoption. And my evenings left much to be desired, with few activities and no close friends with whom to socialize. On weekends my husband and I got out for an occasional hike, but we spent a lot of time working on our 100-year-old house. I felt very socially isolated.

In late October, I convinced my husband to attend an event in Denver called the Witches' Ball. We dressed in spooky attire and went to the

Masonic Hall where we gawked at the costumes and watched a fantastic performance by a belly dance group called Serpent Moon. I had so much fun and went home to look up the group's web page. I found that they all taught dance classes and I vowed to join, but kept putting it off until after the holidays.

When I finally walked into class, the women were all very friendly and I got a positive vibe from the group. Although I hadn't danced regularly in quite some time, I found my skill level adequate and I was welcomed to the group and immediately swept up in plans for performances.

Denise joined the group around the same time. She was also a transplant to Denver and didn't have a robust social circle here. We hit it off and I felt a kinship with her, but I hesitated to get close too quickly. I had a history of forming friendships of convenience when I was lonely, only to find later that my new friend and I were not as compatible for close friendship as I thought. The results were sometimes awkward and I did not want to make the same mistake again and cause any uncomfortable situations that would jeopardize my participation in this new group.

But as time went by, Denise and I found we did have much in common. We had similar likes and a quirky sense of humor. We chatted during class, made some costume shopping trips together, and finally ended up having a semi-regular movie night with our spouses at a local theater.

When I found out I was pregnant with my son, I was giddy. I opted to tell my dance troupe early because my health had become a cause for some concern, and I wanted them to know the happy reason for my recent fatigue and other health issues. Denise and the rest of the women were so excited for me. They loved to hear the details each week about how big my baby was and how he was developing. Together they threw me the most beautiful and memorable birth circle and baby shower. Since my own family members were all so far away, I was touched to have my dance sisters looking out for me and sharing the excitement of my pregnancy.

The day my son was born, Denise and her husband Kevin visited us in the hospital. They were the first people besides the hospital staff, my husband, and me to hold the new baby. I still cherish those pictures and they are displayed prominently on our "friends and family" wall in our home.

Throughout those hazy first weeks as a new mom, I lost touch with most of my pre-baby friends, but Denise continued to visit. She held the baby, kept me company, told me stories about the dance troupe, and gave me a lifeline to the world outside our sleep-deprived but deliriously happy home.

Later, I tried to return to dance class, eager for exercise, companionship and a chance to recapture some small part of my pre-baby life. But then my son went through a difficult period of nap boycotts and crankiness which caused me to hide out at home for fear of making a public scene. In the evenings, even though my husband was willing to watch the baby, I was physically and emotionally wiped out and couldn't find the energy to make myself go to dance class. I again felt socially isolated and depressed.

Denise continued to visit, usually appearing on my doorstep with a soy chai latte and no expectations for the day except to hang out and keep us company. Her presence brought smiles and laughter to my otherwise stressed and harried days and helped me feel like I still had some connection to my pre-baby life and identity. When she left, she would give me a hug and tell me how much fun she had.

Now that my son is older and easier to parent, I have found some time to re-join my dance troupe. I am looking forward to my first performance with them in almost a year and I can't wait for the thrill of being up there on stage again with my "sole" sisters. They never gave up on me, especially Denise, even when I was lost in the fog of new motherhood. And they all welcomed me back with open arms when I was ready.

Hollie Deline is a former computer programmer for Best Friends Animal Society and a current stay-at-home mom. Her hobbies include taking photos of her son and two cats, and occasionally of nature when she is allowed out of the house. She enjoys cooking when she doesn't have a toddler hanging on her leg and sometimes when she does, and she loves to belly dance, which she could not manage without her incredibly supportive husband.

Vulnerable and Open To A New Life

KIMBERLY BITHER

After 15 years of marriage, and two children, my husband asked for a divorce. I was in an unhappy marriage, with years of arguing and failed communication. But I was holding tight to the ideal that a good mother stays married, supports her husband, and keeps her family together no matter what, even though I desperately wanted out.

I can't remember the first person I confided in, or exactly when it was, but when your marriage ends you can't keep it a secret; you're forced to tell people. When I started opening up to my friends and neighbors, everyone was in shock. They had no idea that anything was wrong because I did such a great job hiding the truth, feeling too vulnerable if I opened up to people. I never felt comfortable talking to my friends about how unhappy I was or what was wrong with my marriage.

However, it was when I allowed myself to open up to my friends, that I realized how many friends I actually have. I began to experience close friendships, which my life has been lacking for quite some time. I told myself this was because I was too busy being a mom, but now I see that it was because I didn't allow people to truly get to know me.

Once I started to share myself with others, I couldn't believe how much comfort I felt from doing so. I began to reach out more, and decided to attend a conference, BlogHer. Being a blogger for nearly seven years, I was excited to see if I could actually take my blog to the next level. It was at this conference that I met many amazing women.

After the first day of sessions, I wound up going to dinner with a few women I met. As we left the Hilton and ventured out in New York City to find a place to eat, one woman I met named Danielle asked me if I had children. I then began to tell her my situation.

Suddenly, she confessed to me that she went through the exact same thing.

She was around my age, had two children, and she struggled to accept her divorce. It inspired her to start a blog which focuses on her attempt to continue experiencing new things in life, despite feeling as if her world ended when she got divorced.

As the other women hear our conversation, they show great interest in both of our stories. The next thing I know, I'm sitting in a restaurant with three women I just met a few hours ago and we are sharing our life stories as if we knew each other forever.

One of those women was Lisa, whom I would now consider a dear friend, although we have only known each other less than a year. We made an instant connection and our conversations flow without pause. She grew up in New Jersey just outside of Manhattan, I grew up over the bridge on Long Island, and I think we have a New York connection.

At first it seemed as if we just naturally got along, our personalities in sync with one another. Along the way we discovered we have a lot in common, as well. We both love to shop, we like many of the same actors, movies, and musicians, all things Italian, and we seem to be able to relate to one another on just about any topic.

But over the past eight months, which has included multiple trips to visit her in Rhode Island, as well as numerous phone calls that can easily go on for hours, if we had the time, I have discovered that we share more than the personality and cultural connections. We are two women who share the dream of living an extraordinary life.

We both think big and dream big, feeling the need to create something that comes from within us and from our passions. We struggle to find the balance between motherhood and our dreams of conquering the world. And the timing of our meeting couldn't have been planned any better, because we are both at a point in our lives at which we need to make our dreams come to life.

She has been working to build her dream through her blog, Lee Lee's Room: Life and Lyrics (LeeLeesRoom.com), which is about her love of

Bruce Springsteen and how his music as helped her throughout her life, including her battle with thyroid cancer. Her plan is to evolve and create a place for people to share stories of how music has helped and inspired them in their lives.

For me, ever since my first job working in a women's health club, I have dreamed of helping women feel empowered in their lives, inspiring them to believe in their potential, and encouraging them to know that in addition to their value to others, they also need to value themselves. I am finally making that happen, as I prepare to launch my first health and fitness club for women which will focus on much more than exercise and nutrition, including a strong emphasis on building a women's community based on friendship, support, and belonging.

As we both try to get our ideas off the ground and share our passions and insight with the world, we have been there for each other, supporting and inspiring one another through our journey.

While many of us have friends that we share things in common with, I have found that in my own life, when you have a friend who shares your passions, those friendships are the most rewarding. It's a chemistry between two people that can not be explained. You "get" each other.

And while at first, my divorce seemed so devastating, I have come to discover it was the best thing to happen to me. It forced me to step outside of my shell and build meaningful friendships that have brought richness, comfort, and purpose to my life. I have experienced what it feels like to have a friend to depend on in times of need, but have also felt the satisfaction of being there for them when they need me.

Kimberly Bither is an entrepreneur, health & fitness professional, nutritionist, teacher, and writer. She is currently in the process of opening a new health and fitness club for women. She has been blogging since 2006 at KimberlyFitness.com *and* KimberlyBither.com, *has been a featured blogger for* Livestrong.com, DoleNutrition.com, Mint.com, *among others, and was a "Featured Fitness Professional" in* American Fitness Magazine *in 2009. She lives in Massachusetts with her two children.*

Friendships and Race: Black Women and White Women

SHAY STEWART-BOULEY

Since moving to Maine, I have spent a lot of time by myself, since when I made the decision to relocate 1100 miles away from family and friends, it pretty much meant starting over as far as friends. Don't get me wrong; I still have some close friends back in Chicago but the one thing that is missing for me here is just some girls to kick it with. Either *Sex and the City* style or *Girlfriends* style since I couldn't convince any of my friends back in Chicago to move out with me and the family.

That said, making friends as an adult plain ole sucks. It sucks even more when you are a Black woman living in the whitest state in America. After a few years the realization that if I were ever going to even have any casual grab a drink buddies, that I might need to expand my horizons to include white women, has always left me feeling unsettled.

Now some might find the fact that I am not comfortable with white girlfriends a bit laughable, especially when you consider that I have a white husband. I will admit maybe I have some deep down prejudice, but the truth is that since the age of 17, it's been real hard for me to get past even the casual acquaintance stage with 99% of the white women I meet. The only exception has been my girl "C" back in Chicago. We used to work together; in fact she was my boss. She can work my nerves but on some levels she is the only white woman I have met as an adult who is not walking around with that attitude and air of privilege that seems to infect so many white women at an early age.

No, truthfully my experience is that most white women are looking for a "Mammy" to their Scarlett or maybe even a nice warm Oprah to call a friend and this sista is not the one. Don't get me wrong. I don't try to be a bitch. I try to give folks the benefit of the doubt, but inevitably on some level it just is never a match.

I know I am not the only sista who suffers from this dilemma. I recently saw *Sex & The City*, the movie and was downright offended that one of the girls finally gets a Black "friend." Carrie needs an assistant and hires Louise (played by Oscar winner Jennifer Hudson...Damn, an Oscar winner can't do better than being a modern day Mammy). Interestingly enough, I saw this movie with some white women and while they generally enjoyed the movie, me, I was fuming over how come the helper, the savior, had to be a sista? Super Negro woman to the rescue, to help restore the fallen white women. At this stage in my life, that shit is just not happening. I wanna know: where is *my* Mammy to make it all right?

Then again, I thought about it on a large scale. Sistas are often portrayed as being strong women, yet white women can just be human, and on some level I have seen that at work in my real life relationships. If and when a Black woman shows emotion, it's like folks cannot handle it so we stifle that shit, which we all know is a bad, bad thing. Hello, health problems.

Even well-meaning white women who try to connect with a sista still get it wrong, since even when a white woman is not looking for her long lost Mammy, the opposite end is trying so hard that a sista starts feeling like a special Negro pet project. Yep, I have been there, done that and that too does not work for the kid.

I was thinking about the 2008 presidential primary season here in America and while there were sistas who supported Hillary, there were those of us who just could not buy into the brand of feminism that her white female supporters were selling. After all, many of the loudest and most ardent Hillary supporters were women who cracked the glass ceiling back in the 80's while keeping some Third World woman of color at home, tending to her family. As a young Black woman, what would I have in common with that? Not a thing. It's the reason that, for sistas like myself, feminism will never appeal to me, at least not in the form most commonly espoused by old skool feminists.

Perhaps white women and black women can one day find a common ground, where white women can acknowledge the inherent privilege they have by virtue of being white. Until then I suspect most white women will just be casual acquaintances.

Shay Stewart-Bouley is a Chicago-born, Chicago-raised chick who was forcibly relocated to Maine in 2002. (How else does a Black woman from Chicago end up in Maine?) She is the executive director of a faith-based community center and writes periodically for Maine newspapers, as well as her own column, Diverse-City. *In 2011 she won a New England Press Award for her writing on diversity issues and has been named one of the Babble Top 100 Mom Bloggers. She can be found online at* Black Girl in Maine.

Mixer, Memento

DEBORAH QUINN

I have a new coffee table. Big and square, it's exactly the right height to rest my feet on while I sit on the couch. I have a new dining table, too, and in the kitchen cabinet there's a new mixer—one of those fancy standing mixers with an attachment for mixing bread dough. Of course, in the two years I've lived in Abu Dhabi, I've made bread exactly three times, so I don't know if I'll ever *use* that mixer.

I bought the mixer as a memento, actually, from friends who are leaving Abu Dhabi permanently. They're going back to the States after eight years abroad and the mixer won't work on a US electrical current. The dining table and coffee table are also mementos, purchased from another set of friends also moving away.

Most major metropolitan areas have expat communities, whether the high-end corner office types or the unskilled workers who clean those offices, but in Abu Dhabi, the population seems more fluid than it is in other places. Sometimes, in fact, living here seems like living in Chile under Pinochet: one day you're nodding and smiling at the nice couple with the little dog who live down the street, and then it's two weeks gone and you realize their house has been vacant for days.

Where did they go with that little dog? Across town? Across the globe? Back "home," wherever that might be? Did someone get sick, lose a job, get a job, have a baby, split up? I feel like I live in a city of unfinished stories and loose ends. Sometimes you get the full story: you say good-bye and all those other farewell things that you mean when you say them: "come visit," and "we'll visit," and "there's always Facebook." But more often than not, people just disappear; we notice for a minute and then life swirls on.

I suppose, on the one hand, the optimistic view of these transient relationships would be to see a web of friendships spreading across the globe and to imagine that children who grow up in ex-pat cultures will always have a friend's couch to sleep on, no matter where they find themselves.

But on the pessimistic other hand, this fluid community creates a kind of tentativeness: why invest in a new friendship if that friendship will soon become long distance? This question seems particularly pressing at my age, which is to say no longer in the first bloom (or even the second bloom) of youth: I'm middle-aged, frequently crabby, often tired, all of which makes making friends really hard. All that small talk and getting-to-know-you chitchat? Really, who has time?

Except, of course, as Simone Weil once said, "Being rooted is perhaps the most important and least recognized need of the human soul." Without friends and the sense of community that friends provide, can we feel rooted anywhere? Are we supposed to carry our roots with us, like trees at a garden store, each with its root-ball tenderly wrapped in burlap to make it easier to transport—and transplant?

I have just moved to a new house, with every expectation of putting down our own roots, and as if to literalize the metaphor, there's a little garden, where come September, I'm imagining frangipangi and jasmine, maybe a pot of herbs in a shady corner. I will cook for new friends in the neighborhood and try not to be crabby. Maybe I'll even bake bread for these as yet unmet friends. After all, I have a mixer with just the right attachment.

Deborah Quinn has been writing mannahattamamma.com *since 2008, when she was a working mom living in New York with three boys (two sons and a husband). In 2011, she moved with all three boys—plus assorted books, legos, dvds, soccer balls, and electronic gadgets—to Abu Dhabi, in the UAE. She is a literature professor and writer—when she's not driving one of her children to soccer practice, she's thinking of getting a professional chauffeur's licenses. She has published numerous scholarly articles and monographs; other work has appeared in* Mothers of Opinion, *edited by Joanne Bamberger (aka Pundit Mom), and* You Have Lipstick on Your Teeth, *edited by Leslie Marinelli (aka The Bearded Iris). She writes a bi-weekly column for* The National, *the English-language newspaper of the UAE.*

From Natural Disaster To The Mall: A Tale of Working Friendship

EMILY MEROWITZ TEDESCHI

Although I seem friendly with a lot of people, I have very few people in my life that I let close enough to be actual friends. To have someone in my life who knows how neurotic I am but also sees the good in me—it is a truly wonderful gift. A true friend is someone you don't have to provide any context for—no need to explain why I'm occasionally a titanic asshole, or why authority figures make me cringy, or why I loathe driving with every pore of my being. Nope, they got this, they don't need any explanation.

My mom was a housewife, who seemed quite relieved to quit teaching English to remedial students in Gloucester so she could stay home while my dad went off to work—he was a psychiatrist and during my childhood, he seemed to have about fifteen random jobs. When he came home, my mom had her duties clearly laid out for her: make a good dinner and make Pleasant Conversation. Clearly, my tendency to Want to Make Things Pleasant at all times is hereditary. Awkward silence? Oh, I'll fill it, usually with neurotic ramblings that resemble John Cusack talking about kickboxing to his girlfriend's less-than-thrilled father in *Say Anything*. Have something critical to say? Oh, I'll couch it in cringing apologetics for so long that the person being criticized will fairly beg to have me spit out what I have to say.

I also, like my mom, have the self-esteem of...give me someone or something with poor self-esteem. Kim Jong-Eun's tailor? Lindsay Lohan's personal assistant? You get the idea. So despite the fact that I endeavor to keep Things Pleasant so that Everyone Will Like Me, I seem to have no problem saying incredibly disparaging things about myself, all the time. It has gotten slightly better since I was younger, thanks to an endlessly patient husband, a good therapist, and possibly some meds. Maybe.

So a friend of mine has to put up with a lot. They have to pierce through my relentless urges to be liked and my endless self-criticism and get me to frigging relax. It's hard work, people. My friend Stacy is willing to wade through this meshugas and for that, I am eternally grateful. We work together and it doesn't matter how peevish I am being, or how weird my family or coworkers are—nothing fazes her. I mean NOTHING. I know we're good friends because I can't even remember when we decided to become friends. It just seemed pretty easy, and it's probably because we both have the sensibility of a ten-year-old boy. My guess is someone used the word "duty" in a staff meeting, we sniggered simultaneously, you know, 'cause it sounds like *doody*...look, if I've lost you here, FORGET IT WE CAN NEVER BE FRIENDS... and a beautiful friendship was born. There just didn't seem to be any of that strain that often accompanies getting to know someone.

Similarly, it seemed pretty easy for our families to become friends. Her husband and my husband genuinely like each other. Her kids think my son is insane, but they kind of like it. And my son is *obsessed* with Stacy, probably because when he visits the office she ululates like a deranged malamute and chases him down the hallway.

To me, there are two essential components of friendship: open acceptance and willingness to be around during the crap. In the past twelve months, Stacy's dad had a heart attack and she lost her house to Hurricane Sandy. This means that there have been a lot of times when she's been trudging through the day, gritting her teeth like she's in an endurance trial—and this is made harder because when she goes home at night, it's to a room in her dad's house, where she, her husband, and her two sons are sleeping on futons.

Now, I've seen natural disasters on the news. I sent money to help survivors of the tsunami in the Pacific, the earthquake in Haiti, and

Hurricane Katrina. But I've never been surrounded by one before. I didn't lose anything except big tree branches, yet I can still vividly recall the terror of that storm, and the complete, unnerving silence that followed. Stacy had to see her kid's Legos and Star Wars sheets floating through her house. She had to see people looting, the US Army preventing access to her neighborhood, and the smell of petroleum and sewage permeating her once beautiful neighborhood. In short, what happened to Stacy is not something that a trip to the mall is going to fix.

So when her door is closed, sometimes I will leave her alone. Sometimes I will tap on it and bring her a candy bar. Sometimes I will barrel in and talk about my helplessness in dealing with my father's slide into dementia. We listen to each other. We tell each other to get the hell out of our office so we can get back to work. We trade war stories. We pray our husbands have no clue about how much of our personal lives we disclose to one another. And yeah, sometimes we go to the mall.

Emily Merowitz Tedeschi writes about failed cooking experiments and triumphs on her blog, Yes, But Can I Put Cheese on it? *A Massachusetts transplant to the Jersey Shore, she has worked in fundraising her entire career, with a small break to get a master's degree in English from Brown University, which has not helped her career one bit but was fun anyway. She has taught remedial English to community college students and always let them out of class way too early. Emily lives with her extremely patient husband and her son in a small town where you can hear roosters crowing in the morning.*

Love Me Friendly

WENDY HECKERT

I am drawn to this poem I wrote a few years ago. This is a sensitive topic for me, for I have struggled with developing and sustaining a close female friendship. I have always wanted that best friend, the one you could trust with anything, the one you could always call, the one who would always have your back. This type of friendship is special; it's different than having a spouse or a parent. It is a unique connection between two women that is empowering. For various reasons, I have been unsuccessful in this quest. This is not to say I have never had a female friend. Just that many of these friendships did not last or would not meet the criteria as positively significant. In fact, their undesirable significance led me to write this poem. I remain wondering if I will ever find someone who "loves me friendly."

Love Me Friendly
I have this recurring conversation
With myself as if I were talking to you
Who asked me to unravel the layers of
Pain regarding friendships lost.
It strikes me as pathetic, maybe even comical,
That at such an age I am still plagued by
The desire to be loved friendly.

Felt like a fool repeatedly as I learned
My title of *Friend* was in fact *Acquaintance*.

There is a difference between the two, you know.
A friend pulls you out of hibernation so you get fresh air,
And won't allow you to become so comfortable you forget
To live; she does not toss aside your cares, even
When correspondences lag.

Maybe this perception is what kept people
At such a distance, an unspoken expectation,
One that became too cumbersome to bear.
Oh, how I wanted to find someone who dared
To delight in my passions, accept my insecurities,
Empathize with my melancholy, and join me in daily laughter.
When I did, was it possible I was not good enough for them?

At what age in life does one stop worrying about
Friendship in its variety of forms?
At what age does one cease protection from
Friendship's potential to do harm?
At what age will I stop returning to this
Conversation where I pick apart the layers
Of sorrowful regret that I do not know how it truly feels to be
Loved friendly?

Wendy Heckert is an educator and researcher with an interest in professional development, instructional supervision, and teacher-student relationships. She is completing her Ed.D in Curriculum and Teaching.

Big Girl Friendships

VICKY WILLENBERG

I was eight years old the first time I made the walk from the bus stop to my house in tears. My "best friend" trailed behind me, flanked by the crew that picked her side in our latest argument. The walk seemed endless as I tried to ignore their stage whispers and hurtful snickering. It was less than two weeks later that it was my turn to dish out the insults and unkind remarks while she tearfully trekked home.

I was 15 when I waited for the phone call from my high school friend who had returned from studying abroad for the summer. She'd been gone for weeks and I couldn't wait to catch up and hear all about her experience. She didn't call that day. She didn't call for over a week, in fact.

I was 20 when my college roommate hooked up with a guy I met earlier in the night. Later she told me she did it knowing I would be mad but I'd get over it because "that's just the kind of friend I was."

I was 22 when a misunderstanding resulted in 15 years without communication with someone who was one of my closest friends and had a starring role in my favorite memories of college.

These are only a few of the experiences I had with friendships growing up. In between were countless memories of laugher, sleepovers, summers at the beach and all the other milestones that define youth. However, many of my early friendships felt so fragile — as if they would break under the slightest pressure of judgment, mistakes or miscommunications. No matter how much I valued these friendships, I often feared the people I trusted would become my enemies as quickly as they became my "sisters."

I was in my mid-20's when I made my first Grown Up Friends. It was these relationships that helped me redefine what it meant to be a true friend. When I reflect back on the Little Girl Friendships of my youth, I can see they hung on the hooks of childish things — friends, boys and the search to find oneself. They were no less valuable than the grown up friendships I was cultivating and they played a significant role in defining who I was becoming. However, we were children and our friendships were founded on childish things and we often treated them with childish care, making them vulnerable to insecurities and petty jealousy.

As a young woman, the relationships I was developing were built upon the things of grown ups: faith, marriage, motherhood, career. Although our own personal evolution is a lifelong process, my roots had taken hold and much of who I was and what I knew as Truth was solidified. At this age I was taking my Self and turning it loose on the world outside the safe cocoon of my parents' home or the comfortable walls of college. I was picking a career, not a job. I was choosing a mate, rather than deciding whether or not to give someone my phone number. The risks were greater and the consequences for failure were more significant. This was the time in my life when I needed the best people on my side. I needed those who would cheer for me when I succeeded, encourage me when I was losing faith, and catch me when I fell.

Just a year or two ahead of me in many things, my grown up friends had the wisdom of experience and the patience of people who had recently been through these challenges. They helped me navigate newlywed fights and enjoy decorating my first new home. They endlessly encouraged through the "we decided to hire someone else" and patiently listened to the "why doesn't he understand me?" We grew to rely on one another for support and the painful truth.

Over time, we became more than friends; we became family. And like every family we shared barbecues, weekend getaways, and accomplishments. But with it also came miscommunications, arguments, and frustrations. Unlike the childhood friendships of my past, though, no one took sides or stopped calling. We didn't gossip to others or cut one another out of our lives. Because these grown up friendships were rooted in authenticity and love, we forced our way through painful and often awkward conversations to clear the air. We owned up to our mistakes and humbly apologized. And in the end, our relationships grew stronger because we were reminded of the fact that we valued them so much that we were willing to fight for them- even when it was painful and uncomfortable.

I was 29 when I had my first child. I was certainly not the first in my "family" to have a child, but he was *my* first child and I was truly overwhelmed. I had been prepared for sleep and my waistline to become distant memories and I expected there to be strain in my marriage as roles and expectations were defined, redefined and redefined yet again. I was ready to mourn the loss of my career and embrace my choice to stay home. What I was not prepared for, however, was the heavy burden of responsibility and the crushing isolation that came along with motherhood. Every decision, no matter how trivial, felt monumental and I knew I just had to "get it right." What made it even more difficult was that it seemed as if everyone around me mastered these skills of motherhood by the time they went to their six-week postpartum checkup.

In the moments when I felt as if I was drowning in insecurity and fear, it was my family — both old and new — that came alongside and threw me a lifeline. I had a wonderful husband who loved and encouraged me, although he was understandably confused by my ever-present tears. I had a mother who supported and educated me by openly sharing her experiences and even her failures. But most importantly, I had my grown up friends- my people.

My grown up friends knew me, truly knew me. These were the people with whom my fears and frustrations could be laid bare. They were the sisters who kept my head above water with encouraging words and even a swift kick in the ass when necessary. They were my late night phone calls, the deliverers of coffee and the childcare providers I so desperately relied upon. These friendships were the safe place for me to release tears of exhaustion and give voice to my deepest fears: I don't love being a mom and I think I'm doing a terrible job. Through every teary phone call and frustrated conversation, they listened, encouraged, empathized and most importantly, they told me I was normal. They were my safe harbor through the storm.

I don't believe friendships like these are possible until you've faced difficult challenges in life. When life is easy and the obstacles are small, any friendship will do. But when the difficulties of life are pulling you under with such ferocity that you can't even take a breath to yell for help, it's only those true friends who know you well enough who will dive in after you. They don't need to wait for the call because they know you like they know themselves. Sometimes they will even keep you above water and pull you to shore before you realize you're drowning.

The little girl friendships of my youth were built on the things of children. Together we rode the rough waters of adolescence. But more often than not we were unable to weather the storm because our foundation was not strong enough to keep us afloat. It has been my grown up friendships, developed in the world of marriage and career and forged through the universal battles of motherhood, that became my strength when the burdens of life were too big to carry on my own. These Grown Up Friendships were built with authenticity, trust, time, selflessness and love- and they are the friendships that will last a lifetime.

Vicky Willenberg is a wife, mother and wannabe writer who lives in Southern California. You can find her chronicling her adventures in raising two boys while still growing up herself on her blog The Pursuit of Normal. *She currently works in Social Media and Communications and has been featured on* Scary Mommy *and* Studio30Plus, *among other sites. She is also a regular contributor to the* Brazos Family Magazine.

How Do We Make Friends As Adults?

Nicole Dash

Have you ever observed the way kids connect with their peers? Five simple words are usually all it takes: "Do you want to play?"

Can you imagine if it were that easy for adults? I can visualize it now. I would approach a complete stranger walking down the street with children in tow and say, "Do you want to drink some wine and gossip?"

From that point forward we would be inseparable. We would go for walks, get coffee, watch each other's kids, plan joint family vacations, etc. Ahh... the fantasy friendship with no complications. Oh, did I mention our husbands would become besties too!

Unfortunately for me this scenario is exactly that: a fantasy.

Don't get me wrong. I have real live friends. Some I met in high school, some in college, and others I met through my husband (those he also met in either high school or college).

The thing is I have never just met a stranger, started a conversation and decided to make a go of this thing called friendship. I don't even know how I would do that, considering I'm fairly shy when I don't know you. I am not unfriendly, but I do tend to stay in my comfortable zone, which is engaging people I already know.

Yesterday, I was taking a walk with my daughters when a neighbor I had never met about a block away came running out of her house. She greeted me and asked my girls' ages. She also had two daughters and was looking for other neighborhood girls that her daughters could socialize with. She was ready to book a playdate and she didn't even know me from Sam (or whatever the expression is). Then she started rattling off names of people who also live on the street. I, of course, didn't recognize anyone's name. I'm not saying I wouldn't recognize their faces, but names? No way.

I thought she was simply good with names until I realized she only moved in seven months ago. I have lived in the same house nearly eight years and I couldn't tell you the first and last name of more than a couple of neighbors.

In that moment I realized something profound: not only can't I make new friends, but I can't even be bothered to strike up real conversations with the neighbors. What is my problem? I'm not some weird hermit that is incapable of socializing. Is this what all my neighbors think? Am I *that* person? Am I the strange lady down the street that has a million kids coming in and out of her house?

Why is it that I can manage to attend a networking event with strangers, but I can't even manage more than a hello and a smile with the people living four houses down from me?

My husband on the other hand hasn't met a stranger he can't chat up *for hours*. In fact, this is part of the reason I fell for him. I so admire this ability (not the talking for hours part, though).

I'm not rude. At least I don't think I am. I'm just shy and I value my privacy. I am not a busybody, and I don't enjoy nosy neighbors. I also suppose there is this element of not knowing what to say or not wanting to be rejected. On the Tiny Steps Mommy Facebook page, one of my readers said it best:

"We moved to a new neighborhood when I was 9. I got on my bike and rode from house to house asking if they had kids my age to play with me. Granted, that was 30 years ago, and times have changed, but you're right. It's very hard as adults to make friends. I think, at 9, I hadn't yet experienced enough rejection to know or understand the hurt associated with relationships. I was fearless."

Fearless. What a concept. What an aspiration. And for someone who still sleeps with a nightlight, potentially just a dream.

So what is so scary about making friends? Is it the fear of rejection? Or the fear that I won't be able to keep up my end of the friendship? Cultivating real friendships takes time and dedication. Time I don't always have. I am guilty of letting too much time go between phone calls. I am guilty of canceling dinner plans at the last second because I'm too tired, or the kids are sick, or I have an early morning appointment. But these are just excuses — barriers I place in front of myself. It seems that I am preventing myself from having and maintaining friendships. And it doesn't make any sense.

I do long for girlfriends who just stop by and are an extension of my family. Friends who know me and know my children and are in touch with what is happening in my life beyond what they read on Facebook. I want to push past the awkward get-to-know-you phase and delve into something real and meaningful, but I know this is not how it works. You almost have to "date" a bit before you develop this level of friendship and dating has never interested me.

Dating takes a certain ease and casualness that I struggle with. I am naturally a little formal and not good at the go with the flow thing. Growing up, my family used to laugh when I signed all my cards with my first and last name – as if my sisters and parents wouldn't know me just by Nicole. We would laugh and joke about it, but being oddly formal is a part of my personality. I like hosting people, but I need to create an invitation, clean, and plan out a menu first. I overthink every detail because I desperately want to be a good host. Sometimes this gets in the way of enjoying the company of friends, which is supposed to be the whole point.

I understand that expanding your circle and developing female friendships is important. I grew up in a household of all women. I know how uplifting and spiritual the right group of women can be to your soul. There is power in the kinship of women. I believe this and truly need this, yet I still struggle to open myself up and expand my relationships beyond my family and a few select friends from my youth.

I am always making goals for myself, so perhaps this should be one of them – make a friend. A real friend. Not just an acquaintance you talk about the weather with or do share for shares on Facebook with. Someone you can be real with and call on the phone – not just text or message via Facebook.

Is this possible? Do grown-ups actually do this anymore? I know this essay makes me sound pathetic, but I promise I'm not really. I just wonder if I'll ever get there. If I'll ever be the one to step out of my house and invite a perfect stranger over for an impromptu glass of wine. If I will take a chance on friendship.

Nicole Dash is a writer, blogger and business owner who lives in the suburbs outside Washington, DC with her husband and four children. She started her career as a journalist and copy editor. She also managed public relations and corporate communications for a national franchise company, but in 2009 started a home-based daycare. In 2012, she began her heartfelt blog, Tiny Steps Mommy, *where she writes about family, life, parenting and caring for children. Her newest business venture Connect Authentically, LLC, allows her to help writers and business owners connect with their authentic voice. Nicole is also a* Huffington Post Blog Contributor *and writes for* The DC Moms. *She is currently using her authentic voice to write a book, which she plans to publish in late 2014.*

What's Old: Family Ties and Early Friendships

Marissa

ELURA NANOS

"Daddy can pick her up on the way to band practice and then her mom will drive you both home afterward," my mom chirped.

I was twelve, and I was not happy.

My mother had unilaterally decided that the daughter of some friend of hers who was "around my age" could take the half-hour ride to band practice with my dad and me every Saturday morning. Not only was this girl an entire grade younger than I was, but she was also guaranteed to destroy what had heretofore been blissful Saturday morning rides with my dad, spent eating Egg McMuffins and singing along with the radio.

I huffed as I rang her doorbell. But when Marissa came to the door, we stood, looking at one another, mouths agape. We were dressed in the same not-too-tight-because-our-mothers-forbade-it stretch jeans, the same cornball graphic sweatshirt, and the same white Keds stuffed perfectly with scrunchy socks. And when I say "the same" – I mean the same. We were even carrying the same black leather fringed pocketbook on one shoulder, with our matching flute cases slung over the other shoulder.

In that moment, we knew that there was something interesting going on with us.

By the time her mom brought me home that afternoon, Riss and I were old friends. Seven years later, we'd shared countless moments, memories, and milestones with one another. We'd cried to one another when our parents had driven us to it. We'd learned to love, hate, and then love boys again with each other's guidance. We learned to drive (her, well; me, badly), to sing (her, well; me, badly) and to get our mothers to extend curfews. We'd enter and exit each other's homes without so much as a knock. We'd crossed that invisible threshold from being friends to being part of one another.

Trouble began when college started. Each of us had been dealt a couple of tough blows. Divorce. Financial ruin. Difficult breakups. Difficult new relationships. Personal drama. Personal trauma. We leaned on each other as much as we could, but there came a point that too much strain and too little time together resulted in a serious distance between us. Ill-prepared to deal with having to work at a relationship that once was as natural as breathing, we each retreated.

I finished college, dated, and became a lawyer. I got my first apartment and lived my life. But I did so with an internal limp. I had plenty of friends, but none ever approached filling the void that Marissa had left. In truth, I found comfort in that void. So long as it was there, I was reminded of what I'd always known – that our friendship had been so special that it had no equal.

And that's how I lived for many years, vacillating between bitterness and plain old sadness. Eventually, I was able to do the stages-of-grief thing and get past my loss. I had a happy marriage, wonderful children, a rewarding career, and even a best friend with whom I'd created an entirely new story. But there was always the ghost of my friendship with She Who Saw Me Grow Up. I'd think of her often. I'd always light a candle for her when I found myself in a church. I'd offer up silent and sincere good wishes for her health, safety, and happiness. I'd cry at my teenage memories. And I'd wonder –- really wonder– how it was possible for her to never have looked back for me. Marissa was utterly un-Googleable, and for seventeen years, I hadn't heard a whisper about her from anyone.

And then, the unthinkable happened. On a sunny day last May, she found me.

We talked, we cried, and we made plans to see each other. As it turned out, we lived in the same state, only about an hour apart. We had children the same age and had gotten married during the same year. And when she came to the door of her beautiful grown-up home, she opened her arms up wide, and then introduced me to her three-year-old daughter – who was dressed, head to toe, in the same outfit that my own three-year-old daughter was wearing.

Elura Nanos is the owner of Lawyer Up, *a unique company that helps law students kick ass in law school, and helps everyone else understand what exactly the law means. She's the author of three books, including* How To Talk To Your Lawyer *and the* Why Don't They Just Say That?: From Legalese to English *series. Most recently, Elura has brought her signature sass and style to the small screen, starring in the reality television series,* "Staten Island Law" *on the Oprah Winfrey Network ("OWN"). Elura lives with her very patient husband and two snuggly kids in New Jersey. In addition to being a lawyer and entrepreneur, Elura is a piccolo-playing lover of audiobooks, Mozart, and movies about prison, and a hater of crawling plants, war documentaries and raisins.*

You and Me

JULIE BURTON

It was YOU...

Whom I told my parents to take back to the hospital when you were two weeks old because I was done playing with you.

Whom I teased and tormented for most of our early years.

Whose hair I pulled, skin I scratched and pinched, whose head I threw a rock at and who my friend and I tied to a chair because we thought it was funny.

Who finally became my friend before I left for Israel the fall of my junior year in high school. And we were both happy about it.

Who, when I returned home from Israel a mere skin and bones, as the disease of anorexia had ravaged my mind, body and spirit, was so beyond devastated that you needed to shut me out.

It was ME...

Who, after a long and painful recovery, followed by leaving for college out-of-state, and then returning to attend a local university the following year because I wasn't quite ready to be away, realized that I might have lost one of the most important people in my life.

Who, when I began dating my now husband of 20 years, came to an even bigger realization that I desperately needed to repair the damage I had done to our relationship.

Who wrote letters, called, pleaded, gave you space, begged some more...for you to forgive me, to give me another chance, to believe in me, trust me and believe in our relationship.

It was YOU...

Who finally let me back in—slowly—and allowed us the chance to rebuild.

Who was my maid of honor and became g-dmother to my children, and allowed me to stand by your side as your matron of honor and become g-dmother to your children.

Who loves my husband like a brother and loves and cares for my kids like they are your own.

Who was one of the only people who would take my colicky son for any length of time so I could have a break from his incessant crying.

Who shared the experience of pregnancy with me, giving birth to my niece six weeks after my third child was born.

Who, two and a half years later, as we were on the *exact* same cycle and I was late, was the one to look me square in the eyes and say, "Mine has come and gone, go to the pharmacy, get a pregnancy test, pee on that stick and call me immediately." Sure enough, you and the stick told me that I was pregnant with my fourth child at age 37.

Who (I didn't even have to ask) would just be at my door, to take a kid or two, or just be with me, when I was so overwhelmed with mothering four children that I didn't know if I had the strength to do it.

Who helped me feel less lonely and trapped when my husband's grueling work and travel schedule often left me alone in taking care of my children.

Who held me and comforted me as I sobbed when a bout of anxiety/depression took me to a very, very dark place.

Who encouraged me to get help and to take care of myself, and told me I deserved to be happy.

Who has missed maybe one or two of all of the hundreds of yoga classes I have taught over the last several years.

Who always has the right dress or pair of shoes for me to borrow.

Who held my hair back when tequila shots and lobster proved to be a toxic combination for me.

Whom people often think is me (and vice versa). And sometimes we just pretend that we are indeed the other.

Who is the keeper of my innermost secrets, hopes, dreams and fears.

Who is, hands down, the most kind, sensitive, caring, warm-hearted person I know.

Whom I love more than words can describe.
For whom I am grateful, every single day.
Who is my sister.
Who is my best friend.
It is YOU and it is ME. Thank God.

Julie Burton is an experienced writer and blogger at Unscripted Mom *specializing in any and all aspects of parenting, relationships and finding balance. She is a wife and mother of four children ranging in age from 9 to 19, and soon-to-be author of a self-care book for mothers. Julie passionately brings together her love for writing, parenting, relationships, fitness and community service in hopes of inspiring people to live, love and parent with vigor and authenticity. She lives in Minnetonka, MN, with her husband of 20 years and her children.*

Pen Pals

PAM MOORE

I know it's bizarre to refer to Jen as my pen pal. We are grown women, after all. But "friend" doesn't quite convey what Jen is to me.

Though our friendship has evolved, from strictly letter writing to intermittent long distance phone calls (on Sundays or after seven p.m. of course), to in-person visits, to emails and text messages, it was hand-scrawled, sometimes sloppy, always heartfelt words through which we established our bond. In each of our houses, there is a collection of the other's letters. In those letters are the stories of our everyday lives and the people in them, along with our insecurities, worries, hopes, and dreams.

Jen and I met on a cruise ship in 1994. She was a sophomore and I was a junior in high school and we were both on vacation with our families. We bonded at the Make Your Own Sundae bar, both of us too young for Happy Hour with the adults, but too old to be part of this juvenile ice cream nonsense. She suggested we stay in touch. The next day we returned to our homes on opposite ends of the country, hers in Southern California and mine in Rhode Island.

I had all but forgotten about my friend from the Sundae Bar when Jen's letter arrived. Enclosed was a sheet of loose leaf college ruled paper, crammed with Jen's girlish, blocky, narrow handwriting, and her wallet-sized soccer picture. On the back of the envelope were a big "S" and the words "Sorry So Sloppy." The following Saturday, I waited for the phone to ring and for my small cup of French Vanilla Dunkin Donuts coffee to cool enough so I could take a sip, while manning the reception desk at my dad's scrap metal yard. Instead of starting my homework, I grabbed a piece of paper from the Xerox machine and wrote Jen back. And that was how it began.

Each week I would reply to Jen's letters instead of getting a head start on my studies in the early Saturday morning quiet of my dad's office, before the rush of customers. I told Jen of the stress of college applications and about my heartache when my best friend got a new, popular best friend. My disappointment and anguish the first time I was dumped by a boyfriend. The drama of finding a date, ten days before my prom, when my next boyfriend broke up with me the morning after his prom. My excitement about leaving for college, tinged with anxiety over still being a virgin. Jen wrote me of her crushes, her sports, of life in a house with two sisters. She worried I would be far too busy to keep writing to a high school kid once I went off to college.

Ten years after we met, we were still exchanging letters. Instead of finding them placed lovingly on my pink comforter by my mother, now they waited for me in the mailbox at my Chapel Hill, North Carolina townhome. Instead of tearing into them immediately, like I did as a teenager, I would set them aside for later. Often, I would stick Jen's letter in my bag so I could savor it over coffee before work the next morning.

In a letter, Jen announced she was applying to graduate school in my city. I was giddy with excitement over the prospect of hanging out with my pen pal in person. When she was accepted to her program, I found her an apartment and vetted her new roommate.

Soon after she arrived, the excitement wore off. We lived only two miles apart, yet we were more distant than ever. She was engaged to a guy I thought was wrong for her. I found it easier just to stay away than to bite my tongue. Meanwhile, I was absorbed in my own drama, dating a man on and off who was much older than me, unemployed and had stalker-ish tendencies. I'm pretty sure she didn't understand that at all. I barely knew why I was with him, myself.

When Jen finished her graduate program, I felt guilty that we hadn't been closer while she was in town, but not especially sad that she was leaving. She moved back to California and got married. I sent a note and a Best Buy gift card but did not attend the wedding. Our letters became fewer and farther between as she settled into married life, while I scoured the internet on my hunt for Mr. Right.

Eventually, Jen and her husband divorced. Despite the fact that we had unlimited minutes on our cell phones at this point, we reconnected via more frequent letters and occasional calls. I moved to Colorado, and Jen flew out from California to visit. We stayed up late, giggling and talking in my futon bed, vowing to stay in closer contact.

A few years later, my then fiancé (now husband) and I attended Jen's second wedding. Months before her first child was born, I found out I was pregnant. The same girl who was afraid I would be too busy for her once I went away to college became a friend I have come to rely upon to answer questions about pregnancy, childbirth, nursing, pumping, babyproofing, and weaning. Though we connect these days almost exclusively by phone and text message, I still see her handwriting in my mind when her name pops up on my iPhone.

Twenty years from now a pen may be an antique, and letter writing an extinct art form. But the girl I met at the ice cream sundae bar on a ship somewhere in the Caribbean all those years ago, who became my pen pal, my friend, or whatever you call the person who has the story of your life stashed in shoe boxes full of letters — she and I will be swapping tips on menopause and mammograms, still picking up wherever we left off.

Pam Moore dreams of hosting a talk show, writing a book, qualifying for the Boston Marathon, and checking off everything on her To Do list. She blogs about running, mothering, crafting, getting lost and found again (literally, not figuratively), and life with her husband, toddler, and five backyard chickens in Boulder, CO on her blog, Whatevs...

I Get By With A Little Help From My Friends

JENNIFER HICKS

Seeing that second blue line on the stick for the very first time was a thrill like no other. We were going to have a baby! We made early morning calls to our parents that same day to share the news. My parents would be first-time grandparents. Everyone was ecstatic to hear that we were expecting.

A few days later my husband and I went to my mom and stepdad's house to enjoy the Fourth of July festivities. We had a wonderful evening drunk on the thoughts of our baby-to-be paired with the magic of fireworks and a night spent with family and friends. The next morning felt like the beginning of another day full of promise. Still teeming with hope and happiness, I was excited for what the day had in store.

I got out of bed and started my morning routine. Pee, brush teeth, wash face. Wait. Pee, lots of blood, panic rising, get Mom.

I didn't know exactly what was going on, but I knew it wasn't right. It wasn't good.

We called my doctor's office and left a message with the answering service. We waited and worried for what felt like hours to hear back. My mom stayed positive. She was supportive.

The doctor was blunt and not at all sympathetic. "You're probably having a miscarriage. Call the office tomorrow morning to get an appointment to come in so we can confirm it."

Confirm what? A miscarriage? No. I don't want to confirm a miscarriage.

No.

No.

No.

I want to confirm my pregnancy. My baby.

I was heartbroken, wondering what I did wrong.

"I shouldn't have run down the hill last night," I said.

My mother consoled me, told me that I hadn't done anything wrong. She said that running down a hill didn't cause this to happen. Sometimes it just happens–for a reason we don't understand.

She told me that this is not uncommon–to miscarry a pregnancy, especially a first pregnancy.

"I had a miscarriage with my first pregnancy too," she said.

Wait. What? My mom had a miscarriage? How did I not know that? How had we never talked about that before?

Fifteen years ago when I had my miscarriage — before the era of the mommy blog where we share in the honest and real-life aspects of parenting, where we connect with others during our most scary, frustrating, annoying and happy times — there wasn't much real or open dialogue about anything to do with pregnancy and parenting. Rewind another twenty-five years and there was virtually *no* talk about anything related to the female reproductive system or what happened after baby was born. Not about the nitty gritty details of pregnancy. Not about the challenges of raising children. Not about the feelings of frustration, upset and worry. And certainly not about miscarriage. Miscarriage was supposed to be a quiet and personal problem that wasn't shared or discussed openly. Women might have confided in their mother, their sister, or their closest friend, but it was generally not acceptable for women to discuss or share the unpleasantries that go along with pregnancy and motherhood. So it wouldn't have been a natural topic of conversation, I suppose, for my mother to tell me about her miscarriage. It just never came up because no one talked about losing a pregnancy.

But there I sat with my mom, faced with what I didn't want to believe was me losing my baby. Sharing sadness and fear. The two of us together. Connected in a way I had never expected. Both of us understanding the emotional pull of a lost pregnancy.

While I was in the midst of it all, devastated and unsure about what was happening to me or why, it offered more comfort than I could have anticipated just knowing that I wasn't alone. Even though her miscarriage had happened more than two decades earlier, I felt a sense of solidarity and relief that I wasn't navigating this sadness on my own. My mother was with me, physically and emotionally, understanding and offering a sympathetic shoulder.

A few years later, she and I would offer solace to my sister when she had a miscarriage. And over the years that followed, I have cried with cousins and friends as we shared stories as they also experienced the pain of the loss of a pregnancy. Although it doesn't provide true healing or numb the pain completely, it does give a sense of peace and comfort knowing that we have a shared bond. We find solace just in the knowledge that we're not alone. We don't have to sort through it all on our own. We have one another and we're connected through our shared experience — forming our own sisterhood, getting by with a little help from our friends.

Jennifer Hicks is a mom of a teen and tween, a wife, cat wrangler, and snarky goofball. She has spent some of her years as a stay-at-home mom and others in the classroom as a high school teacher. She writes about the good, the bad, the ugly and, sometimes, the very funny at Real Life Parenting. *She has contributed to* Parents Space *and was selected for the Top 13 in Blogger Idol 2013.*

Birds of a Feather Flock Together

ALEXA BIGWARFE

We could not have asked for a more beautiful weekend to get away to the beach. It was breezy and a little cool, but the sun warmed our skin as we sat and enjoyed the sounds of the ocean water crashing into the beach. I stayed behind the group a little bit as I watched my son perform his Samurai moves against the inbound waves. I had to remind him to keep up with the group as we strolled down the beach. My youngest, strapped on my back, cooed and squealed at every bird she saw. If a dog came near she squealed and jumped in excitement. And my three -year-old middle child ran ahead with the "bigger girls," the eight- and eleven-year-old daughters of two of my friends.

Although we have been friends for more than 30 years (though I was the last to join the group, so it's only been 24 years for me), this was the first time (since "First Week" at the beach the summer after we graduated high school) that almost the entire group was able to come together for a weekend away. Not everyone brought their children, but I was glad I had mine here as I watched them enjoy the magnificence of the beach and chilly ocean water.

I saw one of my friends pick my daughter Ella up and swing her around in a circle, causing Ella to giggle with delight. It warmed my heart to walk behind them all, in awe that over all these years, our friendship still meant enough to all of us to make the time to gather together. Mara left her three children with her husband in Chicago and flew in. Priya caught a flight from New York. Leila left her husband with her sick puppy at the emergency vet and came down anyway. Looking around at the group of us smiling and walking together down the beach, I realized that no matter what, our friendship is a priority to all of us.

I would have never guessed when I met all of these girls twenty some years ago, that in 2013, we would be spending a wonderful, relaxing weekend at the beach together, basking in the sun, talking about life, and starting to plan a getaway trip for our 40 th birthdays.

I still remember walking into Mrs. Cooley's French class that first day of seventh grade. We had just moved to South Carolina the summer of 1989 and I knew no one. As the guidance counselor introduced me to the class as a new student, I looked shyly at my feet. Everyone else had already chosen a seat, and it was obvious that they were clustered with their friends. I heard some giggles and assumed they were laughing at me.

Slowly, I made my way to the empty desk at the back of a row, and scrunched down in my seat, embarrassed at being the center of attention.

I stole furtive glances around the class while Mrs. Cooley began an introduction to the French language. The girls dressed differently here. We had moved here from Germany, and although I had gone to school on an American base, the fashion styles were not at all similar. I felt out of place in my jeans and t-shirt and lack of pretty bow in my hair.

The girl in front of me turned around and smiled a warm smile at me. "I'm Elizabeth," she whispered. I smiled at her, grateful for the warm greeting.

It took some time to become an established member of this group, because they had all been friends since preschool, but as time went on, I grew on them, and they on me.

High school came and went. We all had our own interests, activities, and other friends outside of the group. We went through phases, like normal teenage girls, where we were closer to some members of the group than others. But we stayed friends.

Off to college we went. We were spread out around the eastern seaboard, but we stayed in contact. We visited each other, we made time over holiday breaks to get together, we took advantage of this new thing called "e-mail" and were able to remain in frequent contact. No matter how long we were apart, we came back together and easily made up for lost time.

I went away for seven years while I was in the Air Force, but I still made time to come back for weddings and special events. And when I separated from the USAF, my husband and I returned to my home. Shortly after I came home, those of us in the local area decided to get together for dinner. We hadn't all been together outside of weddings and special occasions since we graduated high school. We (legally) enjoyed adult beverages together and roared with laughter over the adventures of our lives as adults. It was so much fun that we agreed to meet for dinner once a month. And for almost seven years we have managed to keep the tradition going. I may not be in touch with them at all over the course of the month, but when we get together for our monthly dinners, it is as if no time has passed. A few years ago, we even decided to give our group a name. We decided on "Birds of a Feather" because no matter what life throws at us, we do flock together.

This relationship that I have with these nine other women is unique and special. I wouldn't describe all of us as *best* friends, but we are good friends. We care deeply for each other, and we've made it a priority through the years to maintain a relationship. As we've grown into women, we have been there to support each other through broken hearts, marriages, divorces, baby showers and the birth of our children.

And we've been there for each other through the rough times. The last few years especially have brought some very difficult times. J's sister died unexpectedly from complications of Lyme disease at an early age of 21. I was unable to be there for the funeral because I was deployed with the Air Force to Oman at the time, but I sent flowers and I hurt with her and for her loss. Years later when J got married, we all shared her sadness of her only sister not being there at the wedding.

These women lifted me up and carried me through the terrible experience I faced two years ago. Pregnant with twins, they developed a life threatening disease of the placenta, Twin to Twin Transfusion Syndrome (TTTS) and I was hospitalized for nearly five weeks before the babies were born at 30 weeks. The girls sent food to my family — I had a four-year-old and an almost two-year-old at home — and visited me at the hospital, which meant so much to me. They made time to go get delicious food for me since the hospital food, although not terrible, was not the best. And when the babies were born, very sick, and one passed away two days later, my girlfriends were at my side at her funeral, and were there to help us as we went through one of the most difficult times of my life.

Shortly after we lost our daughter, Elizabeth's sister, who had been fighting ovarian cancer for seven years, lost the fight. It was terribly difficult for Elizabeth to say goodbye to her only sister. We all stood by her family as we said goodbye to one of the sweetest, most caring women I have ever known. And then when Elizabeth's mother passed away unexpectedly just five months later, once again, these women, despite having families and busy schedules, all rallied around Elizabeth and did our best to provide comfort and love to her as she was destroyed by this devastating blow.

It has become a tradition for our group of friends to make a trip to Greenville, SC each year in September for the "Handbags for Hope" fundraiser for ovarian cancer. Last year, since Elizabeth's mother had just passed away, she did not feel up to going. But that did not stop several of the girls from going anyway. And this September, all of us who were could, made the trip with Elizabeth, and held her close as she survived her first "Handbags for Hope" since her sister and her mother passed away. It was an emotional, yet hopeful evening. As I stood with my girlfriends while we enjoyed the entertaining live auction, I realized what a special bond we have, and how unique it is for us to stay together and to continue to come together and support each other across the miles and across the years.

We decided this year to add a weekend away together, and J offered up her family's beach houses. We found a weekend that almost everyone could make work and the planning began. All but three of the group were able to attend, and while we missed them, we understood that life doesn't always allow us to get away.

And it was during this weekend with these ladies that it really occurred to me how magnificent this relationship is. We took a group picture and Elizabeth posted it to Facebook, entitled "From 6 to 36." And I'm looking forward to the day that we post the "6 to 76."

Elizabeth, Jennifer, Mara, Leila, Danielle, Priya, Jennifer D., Liz, Rebecca. These ladies are special. They are my childhood friends and my forever friends.

Alexa Bigwarfe is the mother of four beautiful children, three on earth and one in Heaven. She blogs as "Kat Biggie" at "No Holding Back" which was started primarily as an outlet for her grief after the loss of one of her twin daughters. Alexa's goal is to bring more awareness to Twin to Twin Transfusion Syndrome (TTTS) and provide hope to other grieving mothers. Her blog also chronicles her adventures as a stay at home mom. Alexa is a wife, mother, writer, advocate, and sometimes political activist. She recently published a book for grieving mothers entitled Sunshine After the Storm: A Survival Guide for the Grieving Mother.

On Girlfriends and Playdates

KRISTIN ALEXANDER

Jenny and I were practically inseparable in college.

Following graduation, we became roommates in an airy, spacious, and just plain fabulous apartment in the trendy Fan district of Richmond, Virginia. But our friendship eventually cooled in the infinite angst and drama of our twentysomething lives, to say nothing of the crippling, year-long bout with depression that turned me into a shell of my former self, much to the confusion of all who knew me.

Jenny and I fell out of touch, only to reconnect years later on Facebook. A little older, a lot wiser, both of us now married, she had already begun her family, while I was just on the cusp of starting mine.

By that time, I had moved away from Richmond, my hometown, but still returned often to visit my family. Yet even after rekindling our friendship, life and its conflicting schedules always managed to prevent Jenny and me from seeing each other again.

In fact, ironically enough, it took a weekend getaway with her family in northern Virginia — my current neck of the woods — for us to finally schedule a long-overdue reunion. We settled on a girls-only outing to the Leesburg Animal Park with our preschool-aged daughters, followed by lunch in the historic district.

Seeing Jenny again, it quickly became clear that our dynamic was unchanged even after so many years apart. Save for frequent interruptions to supervise our easily-distracted offspring, the conversation flowed easily. And later, standing in a quiet parking deck preparing to once again go our separate ways, we exchanged a parting hug that erased any trace of bitterness that may have lingered from our tumultuous past. A trifle tighter and a few seconds longer than your average embrace, this one seemed to channel a mutual unspoken message: *I've missed you.*

But even more surreal than rediscovering the rapport Jenny and I once shared was watching our children form their own. Despite being almost a year younger, my daughter, Vivian, stood grinning eye-to-eye with Jenny's mini-me, Jillian, upon meeting her for the first time. The two girls had run toward each other, stopping only inches apart before impulsively throwing their arms around each other in an enthusiastic bear hug. Then it was over, each of them ready to move on to the day at hand.

That's so Jenny and me. We always did like our personal space.

But it was a picture of both girls riding a seesaw at the park's playground, with a suave, faux-hawked little dude in bright orange shorts idling squarely between them, which truly captured the proverbial passing of the torch of friendship from one generation to the next. We're not sure who the little guy was or why he chose to photo bomb our happy sandbox moment; as one Facebook friend put it, "Hands in the pants, makin' the scene with the ladies. I don't usually ride the teeter-totter, but when I do it's with my orange pants on."

But it was my dad who perhaps offered the most hilariously accurate assessment of the scene:

"Little has changed," he said. "Used to be Kristin and Jenny at a bar with some strange dude hitting on them. Now it's Vivian and Jillian at a playground with some strange dude hitting on them. In both cases, strange dude had no clue what he was up against."

As Jenny noted, there is a lot of truth in that statement.

Following this brief but telling glimpse into our daughters' teenage years, Jenny and I found ourselves craving a glass of wine over lunch. So, we sought out the most kid-friendly restaurant we could find in Leesburg's posh downtown district that still maintained a decent wine list. Which is to say it had a children's menu. Otherwise, nothing about Lightfoot Restaurant – with its art deco-inspired hipster decor and life-size wax butler at the hostess stand that scared the bejeesus out of Vivian – screamed kid-friendly.

It was already well past Vivian's nap time, and here she had not yet eaten lunch. And on top of that, there was a wait.

Jenny and I sat up camp at the bar and proceeded to take turns dutifully leading our children to the bathroom to go potty and wash hands before being shown to our table. Oh, how the mighty have fallen.

The entire scenario had disaster written all over it. But both girls were remarkably well-behaved, even as they exuded a sort of bored nonchalance – not unlike that which Jenny and I easily re-adapted from our aforementioned bar days as we sat alongside them, gabbing and gossiping and sipping our wine.

There is no pride on earth quite like the maternal gratification of witnessing your child behaving beautifully at a restaurant. Especially when said child is tired, hungry, and only tolerating this bullshit because Mommy and her friend were desperately in need of some grown-up time.

It's hard to say whether this particular play date was more for the benefit of mother or daughter. But given their penchant for fine dining and the way they attract the cute boys, it's safe to say that going forward our girls are welcome to join Jenny and me on *our* play dates anytime.

Well... *most* of the time.

A native of Richmond, Virginia, Kristin Alexander is a recovering city girl now living a decidedly more rural life in West Virginia's eastern panhandle – or as she likes to spin it, the far western suburbs of D.C. Kristin was selected as one of BlogHer's 2013 Voices of the Year in the Humor category and proudly took part in the 2013 production of Listen to Your Mother D.C. She has also contributed to online publications RichmondMom.com *and* In the Powder Room, *and was published in the 2012 anthology* A Very Virginia Christmas: Stories and Traditions *(Parke Press).*

My Sister, My Friend

KATE HALL

I was seven years old, sitting in a white-walled room with brown-flecked tiles in a bright orange plastic bucket seat. An almost offensive antiseptic smell lingered in the air as Archie yelled at his son-in-law, Meathead, on the TV above me. I was waiting. Waiting with my dad for my sister to be born.

The next day I was late for school. I gave the secretary a note that said my mother was in labor. I had no idea what "labor" meant. I just knew my mom was pushing out a playmate for me.

Later that day I stood in front of a glass looking at my new baby sister, swath of jet-black hair upon her tiny, red and wrinkled head. I never understood why it was "jet" black, but that's how my mom referred to it over and over. My parents named her Melissa.

Sometimes when Melissa was a baby, my mom let her cry herself to sleep. I hid in the bathroom and cried and cried along with her, feeling the pain of her sobs.

When I was a pre-teen and Melissa was five with a personality resembling Ramona Quimby, I often had my friends over for sleepovers. She would sneak down the stairs and eavesdrop. We'd hear a giggle and I would storm after her saying, "MoooOOONSTERRRRRSS!" over and over again until she got scared and scrambled back up the stairs.

One time when she was in safety patrol in grade school, I went to her street corner and berated her, called her names, and (probably) hit her in front of her friends. I made her look small. I bullied her. I was sometimes cruel.

When I was able to drive, we took the large head of an old doll and locked it between the glass and car top of my mom's moon roof of her Ford Escort station wagon. We drove around town with the head sticking out like a giant hood ornament on top of the car. We thought we were hilarious.

During the summers when I was in college, I was an assistant tennis instructor at a tennis camp for grade-school kids. Melissa was in the camp. I typically lowered my maturity level a few years whenever we were together. We took the kids on a field trip to a tennis tournament and Melissa and I sat in the back of the bus and blew fart noises on our arms and laughed and laughed.

One time, my mom and stepfather went to Colorado and left us home alone together. Aside from me throwing a party, one night Melissa and I got into a fight. I ran out of the house because she was chasing me, probably with a large object. Once I was out, she slammed the door and locked it. I had to walk up to the street to the pay phone to make a collect call to my dad so he could call her and make her let me back in.

I moved away from home to a job in Ohio after college. The day I moved, my mom and sister crawled onto the bed I left behind and cried with each other. They said it felt like I had died.

In the summer of 1998, I was living outside of Chicago in a little one-bedroom apartment. My dad and stepmom brought Melissa to stay with me for a month. After that month, she was to go back home to Virginia to start her next year of college. Instead, she got a job and lived in my dining room for six months.

I remember lying in the floor of our living room, holding the video camera above our heads, just talking. As fond as that memory is, I hope she burned that tape because I'm sure I said something incriminating, or at the very least, extremely stupid.

We finally moved into a two-bedroom apartment and lived together until I got married in 2002.

As adults we've been blessed to have our kids grow up together. Her daughter, Fleurette, is nine months older than my oldest, Sheehan.

One of the greatest blessings in my life is having my sister as my friend. I love having someone to reminisce with and laugh at memories with. We have so many shared experiences from childhood, up through adulthood. She knows where I come from because she's been there. I would even call our friendship therapeutic.

Melissa has been one of my greatest encouragers in my writing. I often picture her as my audience. She reads my blog regularly and later will tell me how much she laughed and how proud of me she is. For the longest time I believed I wasn't funny except for when I was with Melissa. I felt like I could be myself with her and didn't need to censor my thoughts and words. She helped give me the courage to write those thoughts and words so others could see them.

I'm so thankful to call my sister my friend. I love you, Melissa.

Kate Hall is a stay-at-home, home-schooling mom with one husband, Steve, and three children, all adopted from China (not the husband). When she's not answering bizarre questions or wiping poop off the walls you can find her at her blog, Can I Get Another Bottle of Whine, *where she strives to write laugh-out-loud humor infused with authenticity.*

High School Friendships

Jennifer Swartvagher

My teenage daughters are currently navigating the social structure that is high school. As I sit and reflect on my time as a student at an all-girls high school, I can see that certain relationships were instrumental in creating the woman here before you. Of the many lessons I learned as a high school student, the most important one was how to cultivate and nurture a female friendship.

Social roles are very clearly defined in the high school cafeteria. The representation of the average high school experience in the film *Mean Girls* was very much on par. I hardly ever bought lunch at school, so I cannot attest to the quality of the food, but I will always remember the classmates with whom I shared a table. Frankly, it doesn't matter where you sit, as long as your friends are with you. Once high school ends, the lines that once separated the tables become blurred.

I wish I could go back in time to teach fifteen year old me everything I have figured out about female relationships. I naively believed that the friends I made in high school were going to be my life-long friends. Looking back, I can see that I wasted my time on certain friendships and didn't nurture the right ones. As I try to reconnect through social media, I realize that there some amazing women I wish I had taken the time to get to know better.

If I knew back then what I know now, would I do anything differently?

To the girlfriends who taught me things about boys that health class didn't even touch upon, I still smile when I remember those hushed conversations in study hall. To the girlfriends I confided in, and those who trusted me with their secrets, my lips are sealed. To the girlfriends who I thought were just being judgmental, I know you really were just looking out for me. To the girls I never took the time to get to know, I am sorry. Once, I let a bit of playful teasing affect me personally, and I held it against some of my closest girlfriends. Teenage me needed to lighten up a little and learn how to take a joke.

All these amazing girls, and the lessons they taught me, shaped my future friendships with other women. If I changed anything about these relationships, I wouldn't be who I am today.

At the end of Senior Year, Maria, who was wise beyond her years, made us a bet as we sat sharing one of our last lunches in the school cafeteria. She claimed that our small group of friends would not have contact with each other in 10 years. I couldn't believe that the girlfriends I spent all of my waking hours with would become strangers to me. If we weren't together, we were on the phone planning our next trip to the mall or movie night. We would always be friends. I laughed as I bet her, but realistically, I knew she was telling us the truth. Of the girls I am still close with from high school, none were core members of this group of friends.

I often wonder if any of the girls who walk through my front door, stay until all hours of the night, and share meals with us will be the girlfriends that last through my daughters' lifetimes. Since I cannot talk to 15-year-old me, I get the opportunity to share everything I have learned with my children.

Less than five years after high school graduation, Maria's words rang true. I still owe her ten dollars, and if I knew where she lived, I would put it in the mail to her.

Jennifer Swartvagher is an author, freelance writer, social media specialist, and blogger. She is best known for her blog, Beyond The Crib. *She is also a regular contributor to* Today's Mama *and has been published in* Mamalode *and* Hudson Valley Parent Magazine. *Jennifer lives in the beautiful Hudson Valley with her husband and eight kids.*

The Transoceanic Gift

Debra Cole

When I first met Alexandra, I had only ever been to Disney World.

I was seventeen, old enough to know I wanted something more from life than the suffocating suburbs offered me, but not quite old enough to realize how vast and brutal the world could be.

My parents were middle class strivers born in Brooklyn to first- and second-generation Italian-American immigrants of working class stock. This was in Brooklyn's B.C. era, that is, Before Cool. Way before. My father grew up in a middle class neighborhood in southern Brooklyn; my mother came of age in tenement housing designed to beat your soul to the ground.

I, too, was born in Brooklyn, but my parents whisked me away at the tender age of two-and-a-half to magical place called The Suburbs, where we had a house with a yard at the end of a cul-de-sac. For my parents, it was a huge step up, the American Dream incarnate. I spent my early childhood on reasonably priced vacations "down the shore" in New Jersey, on beaches with boardwalk vendors that hawked frozen custard and carousel rides. We always rented the same little house with the coveted yellow bedspread in the guest room. It was all we knew, all my parents could afford.

By the time I was seven, my dad's career had begun taking off, and we took our first family trip to Disney World in Orlando. My three-year-old sister and I loved it. What child wouldn't? I suspect now that my parents loved it more than we did, because they were giving us the experience they never had. And so for most of the next ten years, Disney World was the big family vacation. Sure, we went other places – San Francisco, Washington D.C., Vermont – but Disney was the main attraction.

My favorite part of Disney was Epcot Center. The combination of futuristic displays – with families, incredibly, talking via video screens – and country pavilions was the perfect match for my curiosity. As a child I played with maps, memorizing not only the states and their capitols, but also countries around the world. When I was five years old, I declared my intended occupation to be "cartographer." Even then I understood I wasn't long for the suburban jungle.

I always believed there was something more to life than Disney World and the Homecoming dance, but I was not absolutely sure until I met Alexandra, an exchange student in my high school during my senior year. She came from Stockholm – from Europe, where, in the words of the perpetually hilarious Eddie Izzard, "the history comes from," – to my provincial little suburb of New York City for a quintessentially "American" experience. I wasn't sure what to tell her. That it wasn't all it was cracked up to be? That she had made a wrong turn somewhere over the Atlantic Ocean?

We bonded immediately on the tennis team over a knee injury I sustained in one of my first matches. I don't recall exactly what she told me, but I remember thinking how wise she was, how much more mature and worldly than anyone I had ever met. Later, she explained her theory on Americans' insular tendencies: "When you go to the beach," she said, "you go to Florida. We go to Spain."

Of course, we had our fair share of silliness – boy problems, drinking, high school drama and bad decision making. (As a testament to the latter, we once accepted a ride home in the back of a van of an unknown person following an evening at the local Greek Festival.) We had sleepovers and deep discussions. She told me about places she had been – places I had never even heard of, like Tenerife in the Canary Islands. I taught her the difference between "beer" and "bear" in English. Alex understood me like few others; it gave me hope for the future.

On the last night of her year in the U.S., we laughed and laughed until our stomachs hurt. No tears, we agreed, because we knew we would see each other again.

True to our word, over the past twenty years, Alex and I have never lost touch. At first we wrote letters – pages and pages of letters filled with girlish script, back in the nineties when paper was all we had – and eventually e-mails and text messages. We spoke on the phone, our carefully timed long-distance conversations ultimately giving way to Skype sessions, just as my Epcot adventures had predicted.

And we visited. My first trip abroad was to see her in Stockholm for five weeks the summer following my freshman year of college. I visited her again in the dead of the dark Swedish winter and in the summer a couple of years later with my sister for her first trip abroad. Alex lived with me in Connecticut while doing an internship at the United Nations, and she gave me one of the best surprises of my life when she showed up at my bachelorette party in New York. Whenever we see one another, we pick up the conversation like we never left off.

I was the first person in my extended family to get a passport, the first to go abroad since my forebears had left southern Italy a hundred years earlier. Since then, I have lived and worked in Italy, Bolivia and Ghana and traveled across five continents. Perhaps I would have traveled anyway, set as I was on devouring the universe at such a young age. But Alex is the friend who confirmed my suspicion that there was more to the world than the four corners of my town. And that it was worth discovering.

Nineteen years almost to the day we first met, I attended her wedding in Stockholm with my husband and my pregnant belly. There is something very special about being in a room with someone who knew you before you became yourself. I toasted to the hope that my son and her two boys might find the gift of a friendship as deep, broad and transformational as their mothers'.

Debra Cole is freelance writer and blogger specializing in parenting, health & wellness and lifestyle content. She blogs regularly at Urban Moo Cow, *where she offers thoughtful analysis on issues facing parents today, with a side of humor. She lives in Brooklyn with a patient husband, an impatient toddler and a neurotic corgi.*

An Unlikely Friend

CARINN JADE

She was never supposed to be my friend. Society looks down on it. Psychologists warn against it. Peers (hers and mine) belittle it. Still, my mother has always been my best friend.

Our relationship has taken many twists and turns over the decades. Never were we so clear about our differences as when I was a freshman in high school. Never did we cling to our similarities as when I moved away for my freshman year of college. I cried for her to come to my rescue when my first child was born. I held her at bay when I needed to find my own path into motherhood. Push and pull, frustration and love, good times and bad times. My mother and I have suffered all the joy and heartache of best friendship.

That isn't to say that at times she wasn't still my mother. She gave me a bedtime, I had to ask her permission for any sweets, and she punished me for breaking curfew. Yet she was always a friend to me. She was generous with her input but never insisted that I act according to her advice. She listened to me cry over boys and friends and life and failures. Always quick with sage advice and gentle confrontation, she is a friend that often knows better than I do.

Unlike most of my other friends, we are as opposite as two people can be. She hates change, I'm impossibly impulsive. She was born the third girl to a father who wanted a son, and I was the first born to parents who think girls are the best. She has stunning green eyes and mine are as plain as Crayola Brown. She's realistic, I'm optimistic. Other than our shared decades together, we have next to nothing in common. Yet despite this fact, we spend hours on the phone talking about anything and everything – just sharing our days, our sadness and our victories. She's the first one I think of whether I have good news or bad news. I would set aside anything to pick up her call. They say friends are the family you choose. How blessed I feel to have chosen a member of my family as my best friend.

People always praise the love of a mother. They say nothing can parallel it. But with two small children of my own, I also know the deep power of adoration for your own mother. My relationship with her motivates me, comforts me, pushes me, and soothes me. The fact that my mother is my best friend is proof that for all I've screwed up in my life, I am worthy of love. She gives it to me every day.

Carinn Jade is a lawyer, yoga teacher, mother of two, and freelance writer/ blogger. Her parenting essays have been published online at the New York Times Motherlode, Mommyish *and* MoonFrye. *Carinn hates writing about herself in the third person, but she wanted me to tell you she loves beer (not wine) and tea (not coffee) and being a contrarian (sometimes).*

Why I Told My Best Friend Not To Have Kids

SHANNON LELL

One of my best friends is on the fence about having children, but I'm not. I told her not to. My advice isn't because I regret becoming a mother, or that I think she'd be a bad one – on the contrary. I know she'd be a wonderful mother and I've never for one millisecond regretted having my children. My advice is based on what I believe it would do to *her* because I know what it's done to me.

My friend and I, we are the exact same age almost to the day. We are Pisces. We have been friends for over 25 years and for more reasons than shared decades and zodiac signs, we are like family. We met when we were eight and for the first seven years, we lived a few blocks away from one another. As a result of working, busy, or preoccupied parents, we were part-feral children. Also, the 80's were a different era for kids. Back then we were given a couple of dollars for McDonald's and an entire day by ourselves to ride bikes, provided we showed up when the street lights came on. We abused and enjoyed the freedom.

We grew up together in every sense of the phrase: we went to the same schools, had the same friends, cheered on the same squad, and liked the same boys. We even drove the same kind of car. I know her family and she knows mine. I know all her stories and most her secrets. I know her better than she knows herself sometimes, and it is for this reason that I tell her not to have children.

Like me, and like many of us in the 80s, she was a Wild Child, independent by default. I was the youngest of three and she was an only child and for our own reasons we learned self-preservation skills for survival. We were hell-bent on figuring out life on our own terms and we made many of the same mistakes along the way. We're stubborn, passionate, empathetic and selfish *fish*.

Today, I am three years into the lesson on motherhood and like a good friend, I don't want to see her falter like I have. Knowing what I know about this role, and knowing her like I do, I want her to know the things no one tells you before jumping off this cliff. I want her to know exactly what this shape-shifting role will do to her.

Even as I write that I know she won't listen, not really. Own terms.

Friend, no one tells you when you become a mother about the overwhelming nature of the sacrifice. The effect children have on marriage, your time, body, identity and circadian rhythm are all alluded to with trite remarks like, "your life is about to change" and, "better get your sleep now." They are true, and none of them explains enough.

No one tells you that what you will give will be all you have – that the Giving Well will run dry but the only answer will be to dig deeper – all the way to China – and even then, it will never be enough. No one tells you that the amount of selfishness you have going into motherhood is conversely proportional to the degree of difficulty. I suppose those things aren't easy to communicate. Cakes made out of diapers and platitudes on pastel cards are simpler.

No one tells you that the wreckage of your unreconciled past will come bubbling to the surface all over again in places you never thought to look, such as pictures of the first day of preschool, first family dinners or stumbling over how to answer a toddler's question about when you were a little girl.

No one tells you that your own mother-issues echo endlessly in your ears like storm waves crashing on cliff sides, because as it turns out, mother-issues are as endless and relentless as waves crashing on rocks. No one tells you that having children forces you into that surf again and again...forever. Those are things you should know, Friend.

But every time, right after I tell her not to jump off that cliff into the abyss, I follow it up with... "but you'll never regret it."

The truth is, Friend – and I know you know this is true – I am a better person because I became a mother. Yes, I am beaten down in many ways.

Yes, I am sucked dry and left empty more times than I want, or is fair. Yes, I am overwhelmed to breathlessness. But what I've found in the process is something people only allude to in platitudes on pastel cards that never tell you enough. What I've found sifting through this unreconciled mess are pieces of forgiveness, shards of understanding, piles of patience and reams of capabilities for weathering so much more than I ever thought I could.

Yes, there is more fear, more doubt, and the nerves are more raw, forevermore... but I am also less stubborn, less adamant, less sure of anything and that has made more sure of everything.

I tell her not to have kids because I don't want to see her at the bottom of this cliff, afraid and forced to be brave in tsunami of wreckage that will resurface from her ocean floor. My empathetic fish's heart will hurt watching her gasp for air like I have, because I know her– she's a lot like me. I suppose in a way my advice is me being a selfish *fish*.

But she is too.

And the two of us, we swim very, very well... even in the roughest waters.

Shannon Lell was dramatically tossed off the corporate ladder in 2010; shortly after, she started writing. Now, in between folding laundry and corralling two small children, she writes at shannonlell.com *along with a handful of mom-focused websites including* Mamapedia *where she is also the editor. She writes introspective pieces on personal and social issues and she tries to use just enough sarcasm so you don't think she's emotionally unavailable. She studies literary fiction at the University of Washington and is working on her first novel. Over-thinking everything is her special super power.*

The Way It Was

ALISA BROWNLOW

I received an email from my best friend yesterday with a picture of a vacant building. The subject line read, "Bye Bye Barefoot."

At first, I didn't recognize the place, but when I read the words again, my memories colored in the empty spaces of the building. The side of the restaurant held a small wooden patio, big enough for about twelve tables. The French doors between the patio and the bar portion of the restaurant were always open, the noises of the bar spilling out onto the warmth and hum of the patio. Pink bougainvillea climbed the walls and encircled the faded white welcoming letters that spelled out "BAREFOOT."

I lived on this patio. For almost 10 years it was a gathering spot for my best friends and me. Like homing pigeons, no matter where we were in our lives (employed, not employed, dating, dumped, happy, miserable) no matter where we lived (every neighborhood in Los Angeles, or later, New York, Austin, London), we returned to this patio. This patio is where we caught up on each other's lives. This patio is where we shared bottle after bottle after bottle of Santa Margherita Pinot Grigio (something I rarely order since, and cannot drink without thinking of those lost days). We celebrated our college graduation together, up in a glass room overlooking Third Street. For a while we lived right around the corner and went there weekly for dinner. I'm not sure it was the best restaurant. I only remember the wine, and the patio, and the talks.

We went there when we couldn't think of anywhere else to go, or because it was halfway in between our respective apartments. We went there because we had always gone there. We went there because we were happy and the night was promising. We went there because we were unhappy or bored or lonely. We went there because the possibilities of life were spilling out of us and we needed somewhere to discuss. We went there because we were defeated and sure that life had gotten away from us. We went there to be reminded that we were young, and beautiful, and could waste an entire moonlit evening on a patio with our best friends, just because.

Place is a funny thing. This is just a building, with walls and pipes and concrete. Take away the sign and the patio and the flowers, the menus and the food and the chairs, and it's just an empty shell. It just is, until it will become something else. We haven't been to Barefoot in years. In fact, I cannot remember the last time I spent an evening there. But in my mind, it is always there, waiting for us to pull up a chair, and order one more bottle of wine, and say, "So, listen to this." In my mind, we aren't that far removed from those girls. Perhaps we could still pull on our jeans and stilettos, the flimsy gossamer tank tops and lip-gloss and slide back onto that patio, into who we once were.

The reality is that our patio days were at least 10 years ago. I never wear lip-gloss anymore (too sticky with a baby). The tank tops are buried in the back of our closets. When I do visit my friends, our talk is of babies and careers and how to manage it all, of next steps and what is worth it. We still drink bottles of wine together, but now we do it in a cozy living room, in our sweatpants, with our sleeping babies in the next room. The point isn't that we would even want to go back to Barefoot. But I always assumed we still could.

There is another place that is filled with memories for us, a quirky bar tucked away on a cobblestone street near Saint-Germain-des-Prés. We spent a few hilariously drunken nights there while students in Paris. It was the kind of place where you found yourself drinking something called "Scorpion's Top Secret" out of a steaming punch bowl filled with candy-colored twisting straws, then befriending drunken tourists and ending up in a basement room of French karaoke. The nights we spent in this pub were legendary to us, and it became the code word that encapsulated our entire experience in France together.

Exactly ten years after our brief sojourn in Paris, my best friends and I found ourselves back in Paris together for a weekend. I was in law school,

A was living in New York City, M still in California, and we would all be married within the next two years. But there we were, in Paris again. We wandered the streets and tried to remember what it felt like to be those girls again, young and raw, with bad haircuts and chubby faces. On the last night, we decided to find the pub for one last "Scorpion's Top Secret." We got off at the metro stop and instinctively wound our way through the back streets, silently following, one behind the other. M got there first and stopped. She said nothing and just pointed. We looked up and the building that housed the pub was literally falling down. The front walls had been removed and the floors were collapsing on top of each other. It was being torn down and nothing familiar remained. Though we were disappointed, I think we all felt some relief. We couldn't recreate our 20-year-old selves, and no night would ever live up to those in our memory. It seemed appropriate, that the past should stay wrapped up in our pink hazy memory.

But the closing of Barefoot seems different. It feels like a flashing sign in front of my face telling me the obvious: You can't go back. That old life isn't just on pause, waiting for me to come back and press play. Everyone has moved on, and is successfully living the next chapter of their lives. And I love this new part of my life, love the grown up I have become. Still, I can't help but be sad at this physical reminder that a life I once had has been shut down and dismantled. I've put a lot of work into this new life, but I am nostalgic for that old one. It didn't fit quite as well as this one, but it was the life that bears the scars of my growing up. Like your childhood bedroom, the one that is too small and too turquoise and filled with things that you no longer need, you still want it to remain the way it was, just in case you need to go home again.

What I am ever so grateful for, and am reminded of in writing this, is that, of course, nothing has been lost. What made Barefoot so memorable in my mind is that it was a place that bore witness to the greatest friendships of my life. The things I remember so wistfully, are in fact things that I can pick up the phone and remember with the ones that were there with me. The memories and the friendships aren't beholden to something as limiting as a building. They live within us, and can never be torn down or demolished.

Alisa Brownlow was born and raised in Texas. After graduating from The University of Southern California, she worked in the film industry until she couldn't take it anymore. She then went to law school at the University of Texas. She lives in Houston with her husband and two children, practicing law and writing fiction.

What's Changed: Tales of Motherhood and Friendship

To My Best Friend On the Occasion of Her First Pregnancy

ALLISON SLATER TATE

Dear Friend,

When I met you twenty years ago and change, I had no idea that the tall, intimidating, worldly tomboy from the Bronx with the head full of massive curls and the legs that never quit would become one of the most important people in the world to me and my clueless suburban-bred self.

But you did, and you are. We've been through everything that best friends go through together: relationships good, bad, and ugly, family tumult, cross-country moves, weddings, job searches, milestone birthdays, existential crises. We answered the phone when it rang in the middle of the night. We have shared tears. We have disagreed and we argue sometimes, but we have grown up together, and I believe we will grow old together.

We haven't done everything together, though. Our paths have been very different. Almost eleven years ago, I had my first baby at a time when you doubted if you would ever have a baby. I e-mailed you with nothing but a + sign, telling you I was pregnant before I even told my husband. You listened to me and my every gripe, my every worry. You experienced my motherhood with me, even though you weren't one yourself. You held my newborn. Even more, you watched me hold my newborn and reassured me that I was still me, that I could do this — and at that moment, I wasn't sure of either. You were sure for me.

I continued to have babies, and you continued to be there for me. You visited my children, rooted for them at their games, brought them Legos, and listened to their stories. More than once, I have found reassurance knowing that if anything ever happens to me, you would be able to tell my children all about me. You would truly be able to reconstruct who I truly was and exactly how much I loved them, and I know you would. It helps me sleep at night, frankly.

Now I am finished having babies, and you finally made the call to tell me that you are pregnant for the first time. It was a phone call I was hoping I would receive, and when I saw your name on my phone, I just knew.

I want you to know that I find myself thinking about you feeling first kicks, or pulling on your first pair of maternity jeans. I wonder what kind of crib sheets you will buy for your baby. I imagine what you might look like, all belly and long legs, when you go to the hospital this summer. I wonder what your experience of childbirth will be, whom your baby will look like, and if he or she will have your hair or your skin. No offense to your lovely husband, but I am kind of hoping for your skin.

Nothing thrills me more than knowing what you are about to experience. I have been waiting so long to watch you receive this gift and begin your own adventure. I want you to know, too, that I am ready. When you need me, I am ready to remind you of who you were when you were 19... and who you are now. I will tell you that you can do this. I will be sure for you. I will root for your child and send love gifts. I will remember the details of you: the songs you sang, the poems you loved, the people and places you have held dear. I'm ready. The best part is, everything is about to change for you, and yet nothing need change at all for us. Best friends can work that kind of magic.

Over the years, the Indigo Girls' "Love Will Come to You" has been my song for you. It was kind of like my prayer for you.

Now, it seems like your dreams are coming true, and with them, my prayers.

I say love will come to you,
Hoping just because I spoke the words that they're true
As if I offered up a crystal ball to look through
Where there's now one, there will be two.

I love you, and I already love this baby. I cannot wait.

And to answer your question, no, you never have to give up maternity jeans. Now that you are a mom, no one will think twice if you have a panel of elastic on your waistband. Perk of the job.

xoxo –A

Allison Slater Tate is a writer and a mother of four children. She received her undergraduate degree in English and American Studies from Princeton University and enjoyed a career in film and television before deciding to embark on the grand adventure of motherhood (mostly) full time. She writes regularly at allisonslatertate.com *and various other websites, most notably* The Huffington Post *and* Brain, Child.

A Child-Less Party with a Child-Free Friend

LAUREN APFEL

I went to a party on Saturday night and I stayed late. This is newsworthy, believe me, I don't get out much. For the past nine years I have been knee-deep in various stages of pregnancy, breastfeeding, broken nights and the exhaustion that attends them all and I am someone who bows to the demands of my body. I am usually in bed by 10:00 p.m. But my youngest children are not babies anymore and a good friend was turning forty. It was time to celebrate.

The friend is a member of my book club, the only regular engagement on my social calendar. Book clubs are the stereotypical outlet for parents of young kids and ours is no exception. We take it seriously, don't get me wrong. The books are read, the issues are aired, it even gets a little feisty with dissension from time to time. But more often than not the conversation is pulled, a moth to a flame, in the direction of our children. It is a blowing off of steam in the most needed way: the majority of us are mothers obsessed with mothering.

I tend to surround myself with mothers for just this reason. Before the party, for instance, I had dinner plans with a couple of other friends, a rare occurrence of having double booked the evening. These friends are women I met in a pre-natal group, when we were expecting our first babies. I remember sitting around a cramped room with them, a lifetime ago now, it feels, sizing up each other's bulging bellies alongside each other's hopes and fears. We talked about epidurals and episiotomies and I wondered if we had anything in common other than the fact that these creatures we were housing in our bodies were due to make their appearance within days of each other.

It turned out it didn't matter what else we had in common. As soon as the babies came, once a week throughout that unseasonably warm September, we clung to each other like ivy. Feeding times, how often last night?, cracked nipples (ouch!), the poo is green, that can't be normal, the tiredness, so tired, our husbands, can they do anything right? All of a sudden, there was very little else to say. My world had shrunk considerably (though happily) and I wanted, I needed, to occupy it with people whose own horizons were comparably narrow.

Of the many gulfs of interest that divide people, children are a chasm. Mothers, particularly new mothers, have tunnel vision. That's understandable. But it can also be boring, tear-your-hair-out boring, especially to those non-mothers who can see the light, so to speak. I hold onto this perspective tightly, because I didn't have it when my first kid was little. Sometimes I hold onto it too tightly. I now err on the side of assuming, if you don't have kids yourself, you don't really want to hear the minutiae of mine.

But that's not always the case. Friends without children support friends with children routinely and, often, genuinely. They coo at the photographs. They applaud the story about how the baby turned over *the hard way*. They make sympathetic noises at the lack of sleep, the cascade of dirty diapers, the diabolical temper tantrums. A lot of the time, though, they do this because they are child-*less* and you are simply a step ahead of them. They are not child-*free*, which is a distinction with a profound difference.

One of the women from my book club is decidedly child-free, but she engages with enthusiasm when the rest of us spin our progeny-laden tales. She was there, at the birthday party that night, and we fell into a head-touching kind of conversation, fueled as much by alcohol as by opportunity. We like each other, instinctively, but we don't spend that much time together. I imagine at least in part because of the fact that she isn't a mom.

Somewhere in between the third and fourth glass of champagne, or maybe it was the fourth and fifth, our focus shifted onto why this was so. "It's not that I woke up one morning and decided," she said. "It's that I've never longed for a baby enough to give up what I love about *not* having one." And then her tone grew confessional: "nobody's ever asked me why before." She said it almost with giddiness, like this was a conversation she had been waiting to have. A successful and happily married woman on the cusp of forty, I understand the reason the subject isn't raised off-hand: who likes to conjure the specter of infertility?

Because that's the assumption, of course, that child-less-ness is more a matter of "can't" than "won't." Mothers can be blind in this way too. Once we embrace the title for ourselves, we fail to see the meaning in an existence without it. We struggle to believe that having it all is not a question of how best to balance kids and career: it is a declaration of not wanting half of that equation in the first place. I fall into this trap myself. Motherhood has become so consuming to me that, despite best efforts, I find it hard not to project onto other women a desire for the sense of purpose it offers.

The party was a revelation in this respect. For as much as I looked at this lovely, child-free woman and wondered if something was missing, I discovered that she was looking at me and wondering the same thing. "Sometimes I think," she said that night, clearly weighing up either her word choice or whether to continue at all, "What could Lauren be if she *didn't* have four kids?"

At 2:00 a.m we left the dancing behind and that question, among others, unanswered. We went our separate ways, back to different houses and very different lives. I would be woken in the morning, too early, by the scurrying of feet and the tips of my daughter's hair on my face. She would be stirred by an alarm clock, perhaps, or by the rhythms of her own body. My day would unfold, for the most part, according to the needs of people other than myself, with all of the beauty that entails. She would rise to a day of her own choosing, with all of the beauty *that* entails. And we would both be happy.

First published in Brain, Child: *The Magazine for Thinking Mothers* (www.brainchildmag.com)

Lauren Apfel is originally from New York, but now lives in Glasgow, Scotland thanks to the Brit she married. A published classicist turned stay-at-home mom of four (including twins), Lauren thinks less about the Greeks these days and more about parenting, the tragedy and comedy alike. She writes regularly at omnimom.net *and is a contributing blogger for* Brain, Child Magazine.

My Mom Crush: Making New Mom Friends

JEN MITCHELL

So I have a mom crush.

She is the mom of Claire's BFF at the triplets' preschool and she is such a beautiful mess. She has four kids like me, comes to school drop off in her jammies, and seems just as frazzled as me. And the very first time that she had Claire over from a play date, she wasn't horrified when Quinn peed on her rug. She was all like, "It's no big deal. All my rugs are urine soaked."

I just adore her.

Now, I did find out that she uses cloth diapers, but I am going to let that slide. I do see the benefit of cloth diapers and to be honest, if I ever had another baby, I'd probably use them too.

But as much as I like this woman, I have realized that the feeling might not be mutual. It's not that I think she doesn't like me, I just don't think that her feelings are as strong as mine.

See, being outgoing and making new friends is hard for me. I am usually never the one that makes the first move. I am used to being the one that is pursued.

Because when I do the pursuing, I come on too strong.

I had this problem in high school with a boy. I really, really liked him and when he finally asked me to go see a movie with him, I was overjoyed.

The "date" went well and we had a good time but after it was done, I was on him like white on rice.

No, not physically but I did call him three times a day, just to hear his voice. I wrote out notes to him, signing them "your girlfriend" or "love you." I sent myself flowers from him on our one-week anniversary.

I made sure no other girls talked to him. I thought about changing my school schedule around to be near him more. I took a sweater out of his locker to wear. I made him hold my hand and walk me to class.

Yeah, I was full on crazy stalker girl.

Now that I look back on it, I am amazed he put up with me for three weeks. Seriously.

He ended up lying to me and sneaking around behind my back. I was really hurt at the time, but what else was this poor boy supposed to do? I was smothering him and obsessed. I practically had us married.

Ever since this experience, I have been really careful with new people. I make sure they like me first so they think my crazy is cute and endearing.

I like this woman so much that I find it hard to keep my crazy in check. But I am trying for the sake of my daughter and her friendship.

I mean, we are only at the preschool level here. I can't have the "your mom is a stalker" reputation until at least middle school.

So I have been playing it cool. I resist the urge to call her once a day. I let her chat with other moms at preschool drop off. I schedule playdates every two weeks instead of every week.

And so far, it's been working.

She has not taken out a restraining order and Claire gets to play with her daughter.

I was dropping off Claire's friend after a recent afternoon of play when my Mom Crush and I began chatting. I was playing it cool and being funny, making her laugh and such, when on the inside I was doing cartwheels and swooning.

We were discussing how our husband both like to start projects but never finish them when suddenly, "YOU DUMB ASS SHIT HOLE!" rang through the neighborhood.

"Sorry," she nervously laughed. "That would be my neighbors."

"Alan! You are a dumb ass. YOU HAD SEX WITH HER!" the yelling continued.

"Nice," I said as we both walked out of her garage where we were chatting and onto the driveway after we heard a loud bang.

"Yup, it's our very own domestic disturbance across the street," she said. "I would call the county police but by the time they get here, the fighting is over. I know, I have called in the past."

I smiled at her, "Look at it this way, you have your ever own live version of Jerry Springer."

She laughed and I did too.

"I know. It's so ridiculous how some people act," she said as again a door slammed and we heard something shatter.

"Well, at times like these the only thing you can do is send the kids out back to play, grab a chair and a cold beer, sit down and watch the action," I said. "It's like 'shhh... mommy is watching her stories!'"

With that she laughed and laughed and laughed some more as I did a mental back flips... yup, we are on our way.

We are almost to the point where I can start to let my crazy show.

Now to find her on Facebook.

Jen Mitchell blogs about life with triplets at Buried With Children. *The doctor said, "I see two babies and something else" to which I replied, "Please God, let it be a tumor" and that how I found out I was going to be the mom of triplets plus their big brother. Often times, I feel buried in children and to cope with that... I tell the stories from under the pile.*

My Momtourage

Dana Schwartz

When I had my first child five years ago, I was lucky enough to have a momtourage. Together we were four brand-new deer-in-headlights mamas struggling to figure out life post babies. For a year we spent countless hours in each other's homes, at cafes, and in parks while carrying, wearing, or strolling our new babies, trying to make sense of our strange new life. We talked, nursed, cried, advised, and confided. Our last time together was at my daughter's second birthday, but we had begun to drift apart well before then.

Sounds dramatic, but it wasn't. We were friends of proximity. The kind of friends that are drawn together because of shared circumstances. Our friendship was intense, born out of fear and the unknown, burning like fire until the flames died down.

I met my momtourage in childbirth class. About ten couples gathered every week for six weeks to listen intently to a neighborhood woman who had not one, but *two* babies (!) and was trained in such matters. I thought of her as a guru of sorts, someone who was supposed to reveal the secrets of the universe, which for our class of first time mamas-to-be was how the hell to have a baby. As the class wound down and our due dates approached, our teacher set up an email contact list. In the weeks that followed, we learned the names and saw the smushed-up faces of the babies who had brought us together.

A few of us continued emailing after the initial announcements, and somehow less than two months after having my baby, I ended up meeting three of my classmates on a sweltering June day. The "oldest" baby was mine, at about seven weeks, the others coming in close behind. Though we were relative strangers, even after our six-hour course, that first afternoon we couldn't talk *enough*. From the moment we walked through the door of Amy's apartment with our tiny babies in tow, stories spilled out of our mouths. We tried taking turns, but it was impossible not to chime in and interrupt each other. It wasn't rudeness, but excitement, and more specifically, utter relief at having found one another. New motherhood is like being airlifted and dropped into another country where you don't know the language, geography, or the culture. You stumble along feeling totally shell-shocked until suddenly you run into another traveler whom you understand, and better still, understands you.

When you're pregnant, labor and delivery seems like the penultimate event, but as every mother knows, it's only the opening monologue to a play that lasts the rest of your life. Those first friendships I forged in the fire of new motherhood saved me from losing my mind, and my sense of humor. Because right alongside the ecstatic joy of having a new baby is the utter despair upon realizing your "life" is irrevocably changed. Like, forever.

Even though we're not all still in touch, I will always be grateful to these three women who made up my momtourage. Names have been changed, but the details are for real.

Hanna

I remember picking up Hanna on the way to Amy's home for our first official get together. I had warned her that my baby would probably scream in the car (as she did most of the time except when she was nursing or passed out on my body). Hanna took it in stride and sang the whole way while I drove white-knuckled. She was always like that, kindhearted and easygoing, never making me feel self-conscious about my colicky baby. I will always remember how she unabashedly sang Old McDonald for the zillionth time to soothe my fussy girl while strolling down crowded city sidewalks, and for the countless moments of kindness she consistently offered, and continues to offer, to both me and my daughter.

Julie

My gratitude to Julie reaches back to the very first days of our friendship when she graciously invited my family to dinner at her home. Her husband is a chef, so considering our post-baby meals were almost

100% take-out, this was bound to be a real treat. But still I hesitated. Dinner hour was my baby's prime screaming time, but Julie didn't seem fazed. In the end, her laid-back manner eased my anxiety, and my sweet yet high strung baby somehow followed suit and fell asleep on the car ride over. My husband and I were able to eat dinner while both babies slept angelically on the table beside our perfectly cooked lamb burgers. Soon after Julie and I enjoyed our first glasses of wine postpartum while our husbands fed the babies pumped milk. It was my first moment of "normalcy" and I will never forget how good that meal tasted. Not to mention the wine.

Amy

My gratitude toward Amy is all wrapped up in loneliness and a respite from loneliness. Just a few days before our babies were born, we met at a local bakery and politely exchanged stories. When she revealed to me that her son would be named after her mother, who had passed away years before, I nearly dropped my cupcake. My own mom had died shortly before I became pregnant, and that recent loss was still so raw. After our babies were born, we mourned our mutual sadness, which was twofold: our mothers would never hold our babies, and our mothers would never know us as mothers.

Motherhood can be a lonely and isolating time. Motherhood without a mother is perhaps even more so. There is something to be said about shared pain, and I will always be grateful to Amy for understanding my loss.

Loneliness might be powerful, but so is friendship. The stories here are only the tip of the iceberg. The rest lies beneath the surface and buoys me up, even now five years and another child later: a rock solid foundation of support, solidarity, and love.

Dana Schwartz is a writer living in Brooklyn, New York with her husband, two kids, and several neglected cats. When she's not experimenting with gluten free recipes for her blog, Celiac Kiddo, *she's writing short stories and working on her novel.*

Friendship Karma

KATIA BISHOPS

My mom recently read an article about good and bad money karma. She called me from overseas, all excited because life was making so much more sense all of a sudden. There's one thing I know for sure, without relying on any articles. I've got kickass friendship karma. Yes, my Friendship Karma can kick another Friendship Karma's ass. Is that where I say that the irony's not lost on me? Because I've been waiting to use that.

Six years ago I've moved from Israel to Canada. Despite growing up in a family of immigrants, there were still certain aspects of my own immigration that I wasn't completely prepared for when I relocated. Granted, I knew it was going to be lonely at first, but I didn't know what exact shape this loneliness was going to assume. My husband and I had each other and two couples of friends who had moved here prior to us, but during those first days it felt, more than anything else, very much like being stranded on a deserted island. Realizations started pouring in: the phone wasn't going to ring nearly as often. I wasn't going to run into anyone I knew on the street or on the subway. In fact, being amongst the masses on public transit was when I felt my loneliest, looking at hundreds of faces, knowing without any doubt that I wasn't going to recognize any of them. And that's when friendship karma stepped in.

My friends and family back home took on the role of a support group, some of them serving as my long distance cheerleaders, others as life coaches, therapists, stylists, and occasionally even as my book club.

And then something truly remarkable happened. I've met not one but five instant friends. I don't want to talk about birds, stones and killing in a post about friendship, but you catch the drift. Friendship Karma really outdid herself on that one. An invitation extended to me and five other women through an online meetup group by a stranger to her house outside the city (with a two-hour commute) did not become an episode of *Unsolved Mysteries*, ending instead in one of the most rewarding experiences I could have wished for. Knowing that I came to a new country and built such strong relationships from scratch was one of my proudest achievements. Stepping way outside of my comfort zone and joining a meetup group in the first place was empowering. Realizing I have Friendship Karma on my side was gratifying.

My newborn friendships created a home for me in a strange country. The sea of unfamiliar faces became a harmless background, a nonissue, a screensaver.

And two years later there was a newborn who brought about unimaginable joy and fulfillment, and a maternity leave that brought about a newborn loneliness. My parent friends were scattered in the far ends of the city, my non-parent ones were incredibly supportive but often busy with work and school and all of a sudden I was that newcomer girl missing her mommy again.

You can get a dog and read as many parenting books as you'll find and you still won't be prepared for the totality of this experience, the overnight not-life-change but change-of-a-life, your new 24/7 job that comes with no training. But once again Karma had my back. Through Gymboree, where I was taking my baby son for Mommy and Me classes, and through another online meetup group, New and Expecting Moms – Toronto, I had instant advisors: amateur lactation consultants, self taught early childhood educators, non certified nutritionists, behavioral psychologists — all of them right there, within an arm's reach, available for an e-mail exchange regarding what to do when your eight-month-old freaks himself out not being able to sit back down, or for a coffee -and -vent session about sleep deprivation, not to mention the same support group back home providing long distance help because babies sleep deprive everywhere.

Being a new mother can be a lonely experience. Being a new mother without your family in a new country or city can be even lonelier. Maybe your friendship karma isn't great, but it doesn't mean you can't call on the

Friendship Fairy or pray to the Friendship Goddess. Either way they won't help those who won't help themselves. If you are lonely, step outside of your comfort zone; take it from me, sign up for an online meetup group and as many forums as you can. You may not meet your soul mate, but you'll find support. Moms are good like that. And if that doesn't help, email me, I've been there.

Katia Bishops began writing when she went on her second maternity leave. Her blog IAMTHEMILK *started as a humour mommy blog, but then assumed a life of its own covering many topics which often caught the blog's author by surprise. Katia also writes about job searching for* Oh Baby Magazine *as well as on pop culture and motherhood for* MamaPop *and* Queen Latifah.com. *Some of Katia's proudest achievements since starting the blog in September 2012 include being named a BlogHer Voice of The Year 2013 and a Toronto Top 30 Mommy Blogger.*

Yoga Bonding

SARAH RUDELL BEACH

It's early evening, and I'm six months pregnant with my first child, walking my dog after prenatal yoga class. Not one minute into my walk, a pregnant woman comes running out of her house waving at me. "Hey! We're in the same yoga class!"

We had been neighbors for months, and had never met. Yet our due dates were only two days apart. We were both pregnant with girls. We both loved yoga. We would be giving birth at the same hospital. I love synchronicity!

We got together a few times before our children were born, but we really came to know each other once we entered first-time motherhood together. Our girls ended up being born five days apart.

When my daughter was three months old, I took her to our first Yoga Bonding class — and there was my new friend, too! I loved these Wednesday yoga classes. We joked about how that one-hour yoga class managed to fill up the whole day — figuring out how to get mom and baby dressed, fed, and inevitably re-dressed to make it to class by 11:15, scheduling naps around class time, then bundling the babies back up in their carseats to get them home in a frigid January, followed by napping and recovering from yoga. That's an exhausting day for a new mama!

And I craved that kind of structure and time with a friend during my days as a new mom. I had a rough time in those first months of motherhood. My daughter woke almost hourly during the night, napped for only 30 minutes at a time, and spent many of her waking hours crying (and so did I). I didn't realize it at the time, but what I took for "baby blues" had progressed into postpartum depression. Despite going to Yoga Bonding, I didn't feel I was bonding with my daughter. Motherhood felt like a job I approached intellectually, rather than a passion I pursued out of love. My friends spent their days at work. I felt isolated and thought I was a terrible mother.

And then at one of our Yoga Bonding classes, my friend asked me if my husband and I would babysit her daughter for a few hours one evening. I felt so honored and flattered and relieved by the request. I was touched that she trusted me to watch her little girl, and it reassured an insecure new mom that at least *someone* thought I was doing things right. *She's trusting me with her child!*

The night my husband and I babysat, I came to two important realizations: first, It is *way* harder to have two infants at once; and second, I really *had* bonded with my daughter. While I loved cradling my friend's sweet child in my arms, my heart ached. I wanted to be holding *my* baby! Even though I'd spent the entire day carrying my daughter as she fussed, I longed to hug and kiss her again and sing her to sleep.

Caring for another baby made me realize how in tune I was with my *own* daughter. My friend's little one took her bottle differently, cried differently, needed to be soothed differently, and, holy cow, could that child spit up!

Our families began to spend a lot time together. Dinner gatherings (which usually began around 4:45 pm to accommodate baby bedtimes), long daytime walks around the neighborhood and the lakes, and lots of playdates (if they can be called that when the kids can't even walk.) But at that age – and maybe all ages — the playdates are more for the moms, right? I treasured the laughter, the conversation, the advice, and the confessions that my friend and I shared.

Our girls grew up together, played together, and spent every Sunday morning together when their dads walked them in their strollers to go to the local coffee shop for donuts. Then the six of us would spend a leisurely morning on our patio, enjoying coffee, sweets, and company while the girls played.

I especially appreciated our family dinner nights together. When my husband was out of town, or coaching football at night, my friend would host me and my daughter for dinner. And we did the same when her husband was traveling. Any mother knows the challenge of solo parenting, and having that friendly support during the "witching hour" of the day was absolutely priceless.

We all say, "It takes a village." We recognize the need to be there for each other as parents. We know our children need lots of caring adults in their lives. But somehow, I am amazed that each evening we all retreat to our own houses, to cook our own separate meals. I want community village dinners! While I am all for bonding with my family at dinner, I treasure the moments when we gather with neighbors to share the work of parenting. I am delighted that my children have many adults — the parents of their friends, *my* friends — to love and support and encourage them. And the bonding that occurs with shared mealtimes is truly special.

Yoga means "to yoke," to bind together the mind and body and breath. Prenatal yoga bonded me to my friend. Yoga Bonding class truly bonded me to my daughter. Our children bonded through their mothers' friendship. Through this friendship, and others, they will always have a village of caring adults bound to them.

As our daughters grew older, we moved on together to Yoga for Crawlers. Then it was first birthday parties. Trick-or-Treating. Second children.

And just when I got pregnant with my second child, they moved away! It was hard to see my mama-friend, and my daughter's best friend, leave. Even the baristas at the local coffee shop expressed their sadness that our little girls wouldn't continue to grow up together.

We still keep in touch today through the wonders of modern technology. When our children get together for visits, even though the girls are now seven, and they were separated when they were two, it's like they've been girlfriends for a long time.

I know the feeling. Here's to yoga bonding.

Sarah Rudell Beach is a teacher, wife, and mother to two little ones. She is the creator of Left Brain Buddha, *where she explores ideas and practices for mindfulness, and shares the challenges and riches in her journey to live and parent mindfully in a left-brain, analytical life. Her writing has been featured on* Tiny Buddha, *the* Power of Moms, *and* BlogHer, *and she is a contributing author to* Sunshine After the Storm: A Survival Guide for the Grieving Mother. *In her free time, she enjoys reading, yoga, and hanging out with her little Buddhas.*

The Crunch of Friendships as a Mom

Rachel Blaufeld

A few weeks ago, my friends took the day off to stand-up paddle board somewhere nearby Pittsburgh on a river. The whole experience looked pretty cool despite the fact that it was in a river . Anyway, my friends — both working and stay-at-home — grabbed a Living Social deal and off they went.

I must say that I am not complaining about my friends in the least, but rather dealing with my own inner demons.

I was absolutely invited to grab the deal and go, but I knew that I did not have as much flexibility in my schedule during the few weeks that they were planning to go, so I did not buy the deal.

Part of me desperately wishes that I could have gone. Again, I do not wish to complain about my friends or make them feel bad as this was all me. I made a choice to change gears with my life, *so why was I being such a baby?* I was tormenting myself over the damn paddle river thing. Tormenting myself.

There is all this talk about moms and work/life balance and personal fulfillment, and, let's not forget, paying the bills. The mommy wars just continue to grow larger and larger. The Working moms vs. Stay-at-Home Moms battle seems to have given way to "working moms with perceived flexibility" to "moms who pursue power careers." The debate always seems to include reflection about why moms work (money, gratification, both) along with the impact of time spent away from children.

The discussion involves anecdotes about what it means to miss the school play or ballet recital or soccer championship for a business trip or a meeting. The lack of time to exercise, snag a beauty treatment, or time for sex typically makes an appearance in the commentary, too. To be honest, I know firsthand that SAHMs also struggle to find time to take care of themselves and be intimate. No matter what a mom's position – working or not – the commentary continues to grow on how to be who we want to be and how to fit it all in to 24 hours in a day, and how our spouses need to be more equal partners (Amen).

In all of this talk, where is the mention of friends? Do women not deserve friendship, or is it not perceived as crucial to our well-being? Perhaps, not worthy of discussion? To me (especially since I have no sisters or sister-in-laws) friendship means a lot. Yet apparently there is no debate over whether losing time with friends — either as a result of career choices or the decision to take care of kids full-time — is a major loss,too.

Sometimes, I feel as though I owe my friends an apology. Not just my kids, husband, or my extended family, but my friends, too. Maybe not so much an apology, but some long-winded story about why I need to do what I need to do for me and me alone. The gratification of seeing my career and writing progress has become imperative to my self-worth as a person. I feel the urge to make sense of why this whole adventure is vital to me, and say, "Thanks for understanding."

In the same breath, I would say, "I miss you. I miss the birthday lunches that I cannot attend, I loved that night we went to a movie and drinks in sweats a long time ago, and I really f***ing wanted to go paddle whatever in the river (but I couldn't and it was my own fault and it sucks)."

I feel disconnected at times from my peers. Why do I never see this mentioned in articles on balance and fulfillment and working women? Are we supposed to derive our only connections through work? Our spouse? Or playgroup? I don't think so. We are complex social beings, and peer-to-peer interaction is a part of that, so in the discussion, we must mention that sometimes friendships suffer and in turn, we as women have yet another area in which we do not feel as though we are living up to a standard.

...And for this I feel wretched. I still love my friends and wish that I could be with them a lot more because I need that. If life were the movies, I would be in Abu Dhabi with my friends drinking cocktails and laughing (*oh wait – that is a movie*). However, there are only seven nights in a week and my kids need me and often I have a networking event or blog assignment and the occasional night with my husband to chat about God only knows what, and well then, I am tired and I cannot always get a sitter....and, I don't want to feel sorry for myself, but I wish I had more time for the girls.

Just as the sadness was creeping over me in regard to the paddle boarding and missed opportunities, my friends rallied around me on a few work projects and scheduled a movie night and a cookout — and I realized that just like the missed basketball game, there will always be another "friend event" that is awesome.

No matter what, we struggle as women to be the best mom, wife, partner, and friend while growing a career, business, or managing our house and it just doesn't always feel right. But then, there are those few times that it does work that make all the struggles worthwhile.

Rachel Blaufeld is the Founder and Writer behind the blog, Back'nGrooveMom, on the intersection of family centricity and running a business where NO topic is off limits. Originally a personal blog detailing her own adventures of inventing a product and starting a business, Rachel discovered she had a wide audience of moms looking for tips and conversation on remaining relevant while growing a family and a business and/or just wanting to find themselves again when kids became school-age. As a true hybrid between a parenting and a business-savvy blog, Back'nGrooveMom quickly expanded to be highlighted on Modern Mom, *and Rachel found herself as an featured blogger on* StartUpNation, The Huffington Post, *and* CorpNet.Com *along with being quoted in* Fast Company.

United Federation of Moms

KATHY RADIGAN

I belong to, arguably, the oldest union in the world, The United Federation of Moms.

I was a probationary member the day the stick turned pink, but was issued my permanent card 15 years ago when I had my first child, Tom. I held my beautiful baby boy in my arms and became a proud member.

Whenever I'm facing a pesky parenting problem with one of my children, I fall back on the safety of my fellow members.

"Why can't I have ice cream for breakfast?" "Why can't I jump off my bunk bed into 20 pillows?" "Why can't I go without my hat and scarf during a blizzard?"

I have found the quickest answer to be: "It's against union rules." Believe it or not, this works most of the time.

My relationships with other mothers have, and continue to be, vital to my sanity as well as my parenting.

Who but another mother knows what it feels like to love somebody so much you feel like your heart is going to explode? Or be driven so crazy by the same child that you find yourself singing, "Brush your teeth and go to bed" to the tune of "Jingle Bells," just because you're getting tired of your own voice and you need a little variety.

As much as I love and value my husband as a full parenting partner, I have found that to do my best job as a mom I need the support and input of other women.

Finding this support was a lot harder than I'd anticipated.

When I had Tom, we had recently moved to Queens from Manhattan, and I found myself a little isolated, caught between the world I knew and a world I hadn't completely accepted.

After four miscarriages, I finally had the most perfect, beautiful little boy known to mankind. I retired from my office job and was now a stay-at-home mom. I was thrilled, but I was also lonely. I missed the city and the daily interaction with my co-workers. The long hours my husband worked seemed endless, now that he was one of the few adults I had to talk to.

I needed friends and I needed them fast.

In those first few months, I used to joke that I felt like a single woman cruising the bars when I would go out searching for mom friends. I would walk through my neighborhood in Queens looking for women pushing strollers.

I joined a gym, took a baby-and-me swim class, went to the playground and the library, but I had little or no luck. I might strike up a conversation with a mom or two, but they usually were on their second or third child and had an established group of friends. They were friendly and polite, but I didn't feel as if I belonged.

My first year home, I went to my local Dunkin' Donuts so often that the people behind the counter bought my son a Christmas gift. He still has the stuffed bear.

Once, when I shared the fact that I was in need of adult conversation to another mother, she commented that she had never once felt lonely because she had her baby for company. I started feeling guilty that I needed more. Maybe I wasn't cut out for life home with my child? Perhaps I should go back to work part-time?

Then I met Debbie.

I still remember the day we met. She was walking to Dunkin' Donuts, and I was on my way home. Our eyes locked, and it was kismet. We looked in each others' carriages, admired each others' babies, joked about our lack of sleep and exchanged numbers.

The start of our relationship felt very much like a new love affair. I still remember our first official coffee date sitting in Dunkin' Donuts and talking for two hours, stopping only because our babies had woken up.

We compared our babies' sleep schedules and discussed how our bodies had changed.

Talk of husbands and their ability to sleep through the heartbreaking sounds of a screaming baby, while we woke up the minute the baby yawned, had us laughing in solidarity. And I was relieved to find that she too had bittersweet feelings about leaving her job for a new life that was still so unfamiliar.

That meeting was the start of many more play-dates and kaffeeklatsches. It also became the moment when I started to feel more confident as a mother.

Soon after I met Debbie, we met a few other moms and formed a little group. Our union local was born.

We cheered each milestone our children reached and worried when there was a problem. We saw each other through sleepless nights, trips to emergency rooms, speech delays, and the Terrible Twos.

Changes in marriages, waistbands, and relationships with our friends who didn't have children were also discussed.

All of sudden the loneliness and isolation I'd been feeling for months was gone. I had found a sense of belonging that I had not really ever known before.

I loved it and so did Tom. He looked forward to his time with his friends as much as I looked forward to seeing their moms.

The other day I was looking over some pictures from Tom's first birthday party, and there we all were—a group of extremely tired but very happy moms. We were sitting in my basement decorated with Blue's Clues balloons, holding our babies, and feeding them their first tastes of pizza and cake.

Eventually we moved from Queens to live closer to my parents on Long Island. Tom and I had a very hard time leaving the safety of our friends.

We all did our best to keep in touch and still see each other, but time moved on, and so did our friends. Our families expanded, the children got older, and soon schedules were filled with preschool and other activities. Time together got less and less frequent. New friendships were made, and new alliances were formed.

Tom is now in high school. He shaves, is taller than I am and has started to think about what college he would like to attend. The other day I learned from a Facebook status that the oldest child in our group now has her learner's permit. The babies that played in basements and playgrounds are now all teenagers who have little or no memory of each other.

But I will never forget them or their moms. I am forever grateful to those women and the memories I have from that very sweet time in my life.

I needed those friends to get me through the baby and toddler years, just like I need the friends I have today that see me through the fears and triumphs of the school years.

I am and will continue to be a very proud, card-carrying member of the United Federation of Moms.

Kathy Radigan is a writer, blogger, social media addict, mom to three, wife to one, and owner of a possessed appliance. She posts a weekly essay each Sunday on her blog, My Dishwasher's Possessed! *The blog was started in the fall of 2010 after many doctors, teachers, and friends suggested that life with three children with a variety of learning issues, including her daughter with extensive special needs, might be of interest. Kathy co-founded the online magazine* Bonbon Break *and is very honored to have an essay in the new anthology,* Sunshine after the Storm: A Survival Guide for the Grieving Mother. *She lives outside of New York City with her family and still finds it hysterical that the woman who didn't even have an e-mail address three years ago is now fully immersed in the online world.*

World's Best Mom?

Jamie Krug

Today, I had a long overdue conversation with my best friend in the world. Nothing remarkable was planned for this chat, and we really just spoke about what's going on in our lives.

She told me about the unfortunate and coincidental timing of her gutted kitchen setup looking eerily similar to one of the "kill rooms" Dexter set up the night before during their completion of a marathon viewing of the previous season, and I'm talking/complaining/freaking out about what's going on with Parker and Owen right now. Parker has Psoriatic Arthritis and Sensory Processing Disorder. Add to that having a brother with special needs, and it's a lot for a not yet two-and-a-half-year-old to take.

Her almost one-year-old brother Owen had a stroke in utero and has Cerebral Palsy. To put it so succinctly in one simple sentence seems almost laughable, based on how complicated the circumstances around his birth turned out, and the equally unsure footing I've felt as a parent ever since. He has a long road ahead of him, and our entire family will be on that road with him. And I consider Rachel to be part of that family.

And then she said it.

Rachel told me that I was a wonderful mother and that she hoped I knew it. She told me that she looked up to me and my parenting. I was so taken aback that I almost simultaneously burst out laughing and began bawling. Instead, I do what I've been doing for the past eleven months or so — I tried to shrug it off. I'm not comfortable with people telling me I'm a good mother, or doing a good job, etc. There is an unease about it for me that I actually can put my finger on, but am choosing not to at this point.

It was different when Rachel said it to me, though. We are peers and equals, each with our own strengths and weaknesses of character, but I have looked up to Rachel since high school. She has (at least in my eyes) seamlessly achieved her goals along the path I wish I had taken. You know, the easy one — in a straight line. My path has meandered a bit — taken a right, or was that a left? A few u-turns thrown in, and a lot of parallel parking. I've clearly taken the metaphor too far, but I'm committed at this point so I need to run with it (or should I say drive the point home?).

She is my equal, yes — but she was always the glue that held me together. We used to joke around that if she decided to go into psychology, her "real-world" experience treating me should allow her to skip her internship altogether. We have been through a lot together. There are things that Rachel knows about me that Scott likely doesn't. But a wonderful thing about the man that I married is that Scott respects this and has no problem stepping aside when he knows that she is better "schooled" on that aspect of me or my life. That there are situations where her advice is more meaningful to me than his may be based solely on the fact that she has always been there and might know more about the history of a particular situation. I will say that again because it is important – she has always been there.

Rachel will give it to me straight, too. She is definitely not a "smoke blower." She looks out for me, but has no problem putting me in my place when she feels I'm wrong. I'd like to think I do the same for her. Honesty and friendship like that is a rare gift. So is someone breaking you of your life-long insecurity-based habit of apologizing to everyone for everything – she did it by telling me to f**k myself every single time I said "I'm sorry" to her for anything she deemed unnecessary of an apology. There were a lot of F-bombs dropped during our conversations for a while, but I finally got it.

For this fantastic woman – my dearest friend – who I love like a sister and respect beyond words, to tell me that there was something about me that she looked up to, well, it made me take notice. Maybe I am a good mother. Perhaps better than my doubts will allow me to accept. Maybe "just doing the best that I can" is enough.

I know I'm not the only mother out there to wonder if she's doing a good job. The difference here is that I genuinely feel that the success and health of my children is riding on it in a different way than the average parent. The pressure I feel is enormous. To be honest, some days I'm not sure if I'm going to crack or explode! Am I bringing Owen to the right therapists? Am I doing enough with him at home? Is there someone else out there that I should/could be having him treated by? Is Parker getting the right amount of therapy? Do I need to change her preschool to one that will be more accommodating to her needs? What can I be doing at home to help her? What am I doing at home that is potentially exacerbating this and how do I know the difference?

When Parker was little, before Owen came along, I remember wringing my hands over whether or not to change pediatricians, the differences likely being subtle between the practices I was considering, I'm looking back now at that naïve woman who thought she had a really difficult decision and chuckling sadly. Now, making a decision to change practitioners for Owen could mean the difference between him walking or not — and if so, with or without a limp. If I choose the wrong therapist, I am taking the risk that he will not have full use of his hands, or speak properly, or eat solid foods before he's five. I try as hard as I can not to think about the immense implications of the decisions I make on a daily, weekly, or monthly basis, but the truth is still there — these seemingly small decisions have gigantic consequences down the road.

I do not want to put aside my partner in this, Scott. He is incredible and is definitely in on all of the major decisions, and about a million more of the minor ones than he likely needs to be. He is my anchor, but I steer the ship. I am their mother. I am home all day long with them, making all of the microscopic decisions, that individually might not make a difference, but as a conglomerate likely will.

I am doing the best I can, and maybe – just maybe – it's more than just good enough. Maybe, it's just plain good. Somehow, though I've been hearing it for months now from other people, hearing it from Rachel makes me a little bit closer to believing that it might be true. If she was just saying it to make me feel better, well, she can go f**k herself.

Jamie Krug is a writer and a stay-at-home-mom with a full-time job as the CMO (Chief Medical Officer) of her family. Her writing tells the story of her family's struggles and triumphs in the wake of the devastating and still largely misunderstood rare diagnosis her son received at birth. She prides (embarrasses?) herself on stating out loud what other women may feel but wouldn't dare say... Her work has been featured on the Huffington Post, AOL, Dot Complicated, *and a variety of other publications.*

Even At Two a.m.

JEAN HEFFERNAN

Before I had a child, I thought baby showers existed just to torture childless women.

Then, I became pregnant and realized baby showers were the one way I would avoid financial ruin if I wanted to have anything in the nursery. After I gave birth, I realized that there are only a few *things* necessary for raising a child and surviving the first year. Most of my baby registry had been a futile stab at preparing myself for motherhood. What I needed more than anything else was friendship and support. I was fortunate to have someone to help me through my first year of colic, confusion, and postpartum anxiety.

The week before I gave birth to my first child, I called my friend (already a mother) and told her that this labor thing just wasn't going to work for me because I was going to poop on the table in front of the doctor and my husband *and then what*. She responded with the best piece of advice I heard while pregnant: *Giving birth lasts such a short time. It's what happens when you leave the hospital that you should prepare for. That's the hard part.*

I was right about one thing. Labor did not work for me and I ended up having an emergency cesarean. More importantly, she was right. Even in my pre-labor hysteria, I knew she had spoken the truth because she was a mom with lots of experience and because she knew me well.

My sage friend was someone I had met at work. Our friendship developed in the trenches, teaching children who led difficult lives, which required us to be on point all day. We could read each other's mind with a look or a tone of voice. It helped to develop both our instruction and a positive relationship between the students and us. In fact, students would tell us that they loved both of us when we were together. On our own, we were just "okay."

Years before she made that pre-birth promise to me, she had her first two children. When she was adjusting to parenthood, I was still single and wild. While our shared purpose grew our friendship in the classroom, our opposite lifestyles made us a good fit for each other once work ended. Her family life showed me what I wanted for my future. I like to believe I helped remind her that she was more than just a mom. My horrible dating stories and drama also reinforced her belief that she had made the right choice because she didn't have to deal with that ever again.

Two days after I found out I was pregnant with my first child, she called me up to tell me she was pregnant with her third. Our children were due ten days apart from each other. The big difference being, of course, that I was at the start of my family journey and she was having her third and final baby.

Throughout our pregnancies, we would compare symptoms and stories. We had a lot in common but while I felt like this parenting thing would consume me entirely, she was calmer, knowing things would level out and life would resume soon enough.

Our babies were born and we started the work of adjusting to our new families. I went downhill quickly and she was the person who helped me the most.

She kept her ringer on and answered the phone, even if it was me calling at two a.m.

"Babies do that all the time."

"Yes, my breasts leaked in public and everyone saw."

"Yes, it's obnoxious. In fact, yesterday she farted so loud in line at the grocery store that a woman looked at me like I did it!"

My favorite piece of advice from her about parenting an infant was this: *I think about the times I have to get up in the middle of the night as a set number. Each time I get up is one more time crossed off the list.* All her advice was positive and motivational. She never tried to scare me with stories or make me feel like I wasn't doing the best job I could.

I would call with a simple question or complaint and because she could detect the edge in my voice or the way I would repeat stories or use the wrong word from fatigue, she would stay on the phone longer than she had time for, just to talk. It would calm me down and helped to center me.

My teacher-friend and I have evolved from that of mentor and mentee parent now that I am past the first rocky year of motherhood. We catch each other when we can over the phone (never at two a.m. anymore) and meet up once a year without kids so we can talk as long as we want about everything but being pregnant and getting up in the middle of the night.

I look back at my early days of being a mom and feel nothing but gratitude towards my patient friend who gave me her advice and time. I can't repay her for that, but I do believe I'll be able to do something better.

My best friend recently delivered her first beautiful, happy, and healthy baby. When I got the news, I told her that my ringer is on and I will be ready to talk if she needs it — even at two a.m. Because, like my students long ago knew, by making ourselves available to each other and offering support, we are better together.

Jean Heffernan writes at Mama, Schmama *but spends most of her time chasing around her two beautiful, feisty children. She recently resigned from a career in elementary education to stay at home with them. She's hoping not to turn her new home into a classroom while she recovers from teaching.*

A Dog, Two Families, and Amy

CHRISTINE WOODRUFF

I owe my life to a dog.

When my husband and I moved to Indianapolis, he was fresh out of law school and starting his first job as an attorney. I had left my teaching job, not only because we were moving, but also because I was eight months pregnant. I decided I was going to be a stay-at-home mom.

Turns out, being a stay-at-home mom in a city that doesn't have a single familiar face is very lonely. My poor husband found out just how lonely I was when he told me I should leave the baby with him and go out and do something. I immediately burst into heaving sobs, crying, "If I had anyone to go with, don't you think I'd be doing it?!??!?!"

Yeah, I was lonely.

Skip ahead to a time when our oldest was almost two. We also had a 4 month old daughter and were living in our first house. Despite my best efforts, I was still desperately lonely. I went to every library class, tumbling class, and park in a 15-mile radius, hoping to connect with someone. I do believe my look of "Please, oh please, be my friend!" scared everyone away.

And then one day, I was pushing the double stroller on a walk through the neighborhood. A dog came running down a driveway, and my toddler (who was normally scared to death of dogs) was practically falling out of his seat trying to reach out and pet it. I looked up the drive to see a woman with two kids. Two kids who looked to be the same age as mine. I put on my best nonchalant face and calmly asked her if my son could pet the dog.

"Sure!" she said. "My name is Amy."

That very day, we ended up staying to play in their yard. Turns out, Amy was just as lonely as me. She and her husband only had one car at the time, so she was stuck at home all day, every day, all alone with her girls. We made plans to take a walk together the next day. And the next, and the next, and the next.

In our times together, I was able to observe a parenting style quite different from mine. I realized that when a child asked to do something, Amy's first inclination was to say yes, regardless of the mess it would mean for her. My first inclination was to say no. That attitude was doing nothing for my son. If I wanted his curiosity to blossom and his imagination to grow, I was going to have to change my attitude. My new motto became, "The messier you are, the more fun you're having and the more you are learning." It is still my motto, and the kids have flourished because of it.

Frequently, the kids would be playing well, and we would be enjoying our conversation so fully that we completely lost track of time. At least twice a week we would be surprised by one of our husbands coming home from work. Neither of us would be anywhere near ready for dinner, and we'd rush to get the toys and the kids cleaned up before we scrambled to get home and throw some food on the table.

This predicament led to the best idea ever.

We dubbed Thursday to be Community Dinner Night. Every week, we would plan on having dinner together, and the husbands would show up at the home of the host family. With this plan, we accomplished a variety of things. First, both families were guaranteed to have a full-blown, real meal at least once a week. Secondly, we got to spend even more time together. And lastly, we were able to bring our husbands into the wonderfulness that was our friendship.

Through these weekly dinners, our families became one. We celebrated new babies, new jobs, birthdays, and accomplishments. Parenting dilemmas were hashed out and plans made. There were no secrets between us. Amy and I could vent to each other about our husbands, safe in the knowledge that no judging would occur and we would be able to be sweet and supportive once the husbands came home. Through it all, there was so much laughter.

We also helped each other through some difficult times. Illness, extended family issues, and death were all made easier by the presence of the other family.

For seven years we made these dinners a priority. Even as the kids grew and we could no longer spend all of our days together, we never gave up on the Thursday dinners. They were just too important to all of us.

And then one day, Amy's husband's office was closed. They were going to have to move to a new city. Every single one of us was devastated. The weeks leading up to the move, we cherished each other's company more than ever. It seemed that every day together was a chance for us to gather memories and store them for the horrible days after the move.

On that last day, I picked her girls up bright and early in the morning and brought them to the farm so Amy could finish packing. We were going to have a full day of memory-making. The kids ate both breakfast and lunch in the "house" they had built in the barn. They played with the pigs and chickens. They climbed trees. They played games. They pushed each other on the rope swings. And I followed with my camera, hoping the photos were turning out. I couldn't tell through my perpetually teary eyes.

We have seen Amy and her family a few times since the move four years ago. We all take up right where we left off, except for one difference. We both cry as Amy holds and plays with my youngest boys who were born after the move. It is such a reminder of the years we spent helping each other raise our little ones, and a slap in the face that I don't have her now.

And that dog that started it all? On the day we met, Amy and her husband had agreed to give the dog away. It was gone within a week after our first meeting. I had been a hair's breath away from never meeting the best friend that I have ever had.

Christine Woodruff is a woman who refuses to make solid plans in her life, but does whatever comes her way. As a result, she's taught just about every grade, decorated cakes, owned a photography business, given birth to six children, and bought a 140-year-old house that happened to come with a small farm. She is fortunate to have married a man who is responsible and sets goals so she doesn't have to. You will often find her either driving their 12-passenger van around town or disposing of the dead animals that frequently litter her property. She writes about all of her family's shenanigans at A Fly On Our (Chicken Coop) Wall.

On Feeling Lonely

ALEXANDRA ROSAS

Pushing the bright green stroller that my mother had just given me, my three-week-old son asleep inside, I circled lap after lap of the closest indoor shopping mall to our house. It wasn't yet eight a.m., but I was already there, alongside the early mall walkers in their white velcro shoes. I didn't know it then, but I was doing the exact thing that I needed to be doing for my mental state at the time. I was getting out.

Almost 35 years old when our first child was born, I had worked outside of the home since I was 16. Most of my friends were from work. We stopped at each others' desks every morning before entering our own cubicles for the day, we shared lunch together, on Wednesday nights after work we'd all go out for tacos; then, literally overnight, I found myself alone.

After years of spending 47 hours a week among voices, laughter, whispered confidences, my life was now one of staying home full time, alone, with a baby. I had left my friends behind at work. I knew that none of my co-workers had decided to stay home after their children were born; they had all returned to work after a six-week maternity leave. *I knew that.* But I had been so focused on finally having the baby that I had been waiting my entire life for, that I never thought about who I would be with when I no longer worked.

Who would I be with? Now, I can see how alarmingly unprepared I was for the overwhelming floodwaters of change that came when I went from working outside of the home to just staying home.

I was lonely, and it hurt.

Lonely in the most devastating description of the void and desolate hole I felt I was living in. 4:15 in the afternoon would find me staring out my front window, my quiet baby in my arms, anxiously scanning the road for my husband's car. I was only able to begin breathing again at the sound of his key in the lock. To this day, the turn of the lock and then the push of the door remains one of my favorite sounds.

How would I start to make friends? I didn't know how. My social world consisted of one. I ached for someone to talk to, the comfort of community, but I never felt ready to meet anyone. I looked a mess, unshowered and in my husband's t-shirts. Any free time I had I thought should be spent in keeping up my home and playing with my baby. Having an infant with colic who only slept two hours at the most at any one time — and then only if Christmas carols played in the background while he faced the fish tank — left me with no time for anything other than trying to get some solid sleep myself.

It wasn't too long before the emptiness that I felt since I quit working began to creep darkly over my entire life, leaving me frozen and numb, unable to smile and worsening the isolation that enveloped me. Even if I were to meet someone, I wouldn't have had the mental energy to string three words together to form a sentence, much less manage a give-and-take conversation with interest and a smile.

But here I was, on this early morning, alone — pushing my three-week-old newborn in his equally new stroller, lap after lap, along with the mall walkers. I talked to my baby, telling him stories as if he were 35 years old; I talked to the air, telling it about the upcoming TV shows I was going to watch. I was scared that if I didn't practice talking that I'd forget how. I was lonely, but I was out of my house; somehow, my survival instincts were still intact enough to shout out, "Interact, interact!" And so I did.

On one of these early morning mall walks, I saw that the bookstore at the west end hosted a Toddler Story Time on Tuesday mornings. I decided to go.

The first day before walking in, I took a deep breath. I froze when I saw no other moms with newborns there. Immediately, I felt out of place among the put-together moms with toddlers that already seemed to know each other and were there with their friends. But I resolutely made my way toward the back of the children's section and stayed for the entire reading. I was embarrassed, both at how haggard I knew I looked and at how desperate I must have appeared — a three-week-old at a story time?? Come on. But I knew I had to keep coming, to show up every Tuesday, making my way past the pretty moms who were there with their crew, to my same spot in the back, where I would lean against the tall book cases and nurse my baby, closing my eyes and losing myself in the sweetness of the sound of conversations around me. *Interact, interact.* Interact to survive, and maintain sanity –interact.

I was lonely. The solitude sat like a balled-up sandwich stuck in the middle of my chest.

I knew I had to find something, some way, some route out of my suffocating existence. I looked through the self-help book section after a Tuesday morning Story Time, and found a study on loneliness published by The Center for Cognitive and Social Neuroscience at the University of Chicago. They found that loneliness has a broad and profound health effect on our overall well-being. *People who are lonely have significantly higher incidences of diabetes, heart related illnesses, sleep disorders, obesity, and high blood pressure.* These are just the physical tolls. There is a multitude of emotional effects as well: increased occurrence of anxiety, insomnia, depression, and withdrawal from others. As I read, I felt refueled by this information.

Loneliness was as toxic as it felt. Loneliness was a force that needed to be reckoned with.

There I was, head over heels in love with my new baby, but at the same time, being swallowed whole by one of the bleakest periods that I have ever lived through. I remember how robotic I felt during this time when I knew no one, as if I were watching my life through a video camera — feeling untethered from any identity I once had. I was alone, so alone, and when my husband traveled, days could go by without the sound of another human voice in my life. The silence around me so deafening that not even every radio turned on in the house could drown it out.

Clearly, changes had to be made, for me and my new family. I had a child now, and he needed a happy mother, and I needed to be a happy mother. And so one morning, as I held my infant close to me, my silent tears wetting his little cheeks, I planned a path to dig myself out of the dark tomb that was choking me. I began by looking through church bulletins and joining their moms groups. I then checked the newspaper for diaper bag clubs at health clinics, and joined their morning sessions. I joined a stroller walk club from a posting I saw on the Y's community board. Since I was breast feeding, I looked for a La Leche League and found one through The Quaker Society.

Whether I made the meetings or not, it didn't matter, I was part of something. On my calendar, I had a place to go penciled in and scheduled for every day of the week. When I had had enough sleep the night before to be a safe driver in the morning, I went to whatever group event or activity I had written in on the calendar. Monday through Friday, getting out of my house had become my new job.

I can't say that I felt that I belonged in every group that I tried, because I didn't. Many of the women at the groups I walked into already had friendships in place, and I often felt like a fifth wheel. Were there sparks of potential friendship at some of these meetings? Sometimes. I longed for a smile from someone who knew me, but what had to come first was learning to find my place in this new world that was now my life. When I was lucky, a bright face eagerly awaited me at one of these groups, but more often not, there wasn't.

I never knew what would meet me on the other side of the door when I walked into these places; I was grateful when the atmosphere was an open-armed welcoming one to strangers. But when it wasn't, I kept my chin up and promised myself to return the next week, to try again, despite the disappointment of being the one there without a friend.

I didn't click with everyone at these outings, but I did make the friends I needed to. Women like Anne, from across the street, who come springtime, shared walks with me. And Carrie from The Quaker Society, a single mother who gave me courage to do more things on my own by setting an example. And Laura, from Ireland, who had a baby boy, Devon, on the same day that I had my Alec.

These women, these once wonderfully steady fixtures in my days, have since drifted out of my life. I don't remember how. I get misty-eyed at this loss because they were an essential part of the fabric I was then weaving of my new life as a stay-at-home mother; they were the golden threads throughout this new tapestry, holding the loose stitches in place for me when I couldn't.

It took the entire first year of my new life to find people to talk to, to have phone numbers that I knew by heart. It was almost fall when I finally met someone I could call spontaneously to spend the afternoon with me at the park. I had survived what I now think of as the most bewildering, pathless year of my life.

During this time, I found a book called *Lonely*, a memoir written by Emily White. Inside these pages, I had just what I needed then: manageable action items to finding friendship. There was a checklist in the book that I followed like a tourist depends on his travel map: volunteer, create park play groups, start a church play group, attend free lectures, form a book club. Emily White's book offered limitless ideas for starting points in looking for friendship.

In the midst of feeling hopeless for myself and for my baby — for having a disconnected mother — there was a light bulb moment. As overcome as I was by my life that was now barely recognizable from what it once was, it hit me, the critical importance of being *proactive* in creating a social community.

Passively hoping for people to come into my life was not a plan. I had to find my friends. My mental and physical survival depended on it. Interactions and smiles with my child depended on it. My little boy needed a happy, unlonely mother.

Through that almost unbearably lonely year, I grew to realize that life should be lived fully, not merely survived. Just existing did right by no one. Friendships, even surface ones in the form of acquaintances, can tide us over during the changes in life, the transitions to a new being, that leave us stripped of who we used to know.

Some people are in our lives forever, some are our lifelines for just that moment that we need them — neither less precious than the other. *If you have to work to find people, to have them be your oxygen during these achingly desperate times, then that,* I determinedly whispered to myself one winter morning while my beautiful son and I walked to our Friday morning Moms Club, *then that, is what you have to do.*

I smiled with the hope that maybe this time, there might be a new mom there, and she'd be looking for a friend.

Alexandra Rosas is a first generation American who writes humor and cultural memoir for several websites. She was BlogHer Voice of the Year in 2011, 2012, and 2013 and was named a Babble top 100 Mom Blogger. Alexandra proudly presents with the award winning national live storytellers tour The Moth. *You can follow her on her personal blog* Good Day, Regular People.

A Friendship Forged in the Crucible

LINDSEY MEAD

I recently had lunch with a friend who walked beside me through some of the most difficult months of my life. We lost touch for several years, and now see each other only sporadically. But even without frequent contact, we are close and always will be.

Our bond is a formidable alloy, forged in the crucible of bewilderment, fear, and wonder known as postpartum depression. We met shortly after our first children were born (five weeks apart, and we improved that with second children born only four weeks apart). We instantly recognized in each other both a spirit struggling in the dark woods of despair and a glimmer of our similar, joyful former selves. We knew that not only did we have a lot in common right this second, but we had had a lot in common in the past and would again in the future.

And we were right. It was such a relief to have a friend like her, a friend who was so unabashedly *fun*, even during a time when we had both lost hold of anything resembling fun. She made me laugh, long and loud, every day. We experienced together for the first time the pleasures and trials of working part time, of growing babies and pureeing vegetables, of nursing bras and drool-soaked shirts. I remember sending her post-it notes with hand-drawn pictures and funny messages on them, and that we both found "If you aren't living on the edge, you are taking up too much room" to be the height of hilarity.

Underneath the fun, there was also deep connection and identification. I've never had a friend with whom I connected so quickly; it felt as as though she was the person I'd been looking for for so many years. We had many points of connection, but still the rapidity and the ease with which we fell into each others' lives is something I still find notable.

I wrote her a letter on her son's first birthday and she gave me a photo album with pictures of us and our children when Grace turned one. We learned, together, to be mothers, and we fought, more desperately than our playful and tipsy exteriors let on, to maintain some sense of ourselves as individuals, as we made this most essential passage.

We strolled for hours, we wore matching tank tops, we went to yoga, we sang along loudly to Bruce Springsteen at Fenway, we drove golf carts drunk in the dark, and we skinny-dipped in the ocean, clothing and inhibitions shed together on the beach. It was tangible, the gradual sense of lightness that came over each of us as we climbed out of the dark place and towards the light. Our journeys were independent but we made them side by side.

We shared wine and diapers and clothing and birthdays and tears and e-mails and phone calls and pedicures and friends and stories and a celebratory lunch for our second pregnancies. I buckled her son into her mother's car for his first night away from her, and brought her dinner and a bottle of wine the day she brought her second child, a daughter, home from the hospital. The last person I saw before having my second child, a son, was her husband, when he brought over a folding bed that we borrowed for a night nurse. I cried into her voicemail when I heard her second baby was a girl and cried again reading her thoughtful message after my son's nut allergy diagnosis.

Our roots are deeply intertwined. Whenever we're together I can feel past and present – and future – overlapping like soft waves on a beach.

The tide goes in, the tide goes out.

One minute we are holding each other's babies in a slew of side-by-side photographs and the next we're watching those children barrel down a black diamond ski slope ahead of us. Those children, now 10 years old, were each other's first friends, and their lives beat like a pulse through all my memories of this unique friendship. Though they don't know each other any more, their bonds endure, even if only in my mind: it makes me irrationally happy that they were, unbeknownst to each other, Harry Potter and Hermione Granger on the same Halloween.

She holds in her hands so much of that first intense year of motherhood, when we were so tired we felt we had sand in our eyes, when we were so disoriented and shell-shocked we thought we would never stand upright again. And now that we are, we talk all the time about that time apart from real life. We miss the wild magic of those days.

Lindsey Mead is a mother, writer, and financial services professional who lives outside of Boston with her husband, daughter, and son. Her writing has been published and anthologized in a variety of print and online sources including the Huffington Post, Brain, Child, Literary Mama, the Princeton Alumni Weekly, *and* Torn: True Stories of Kids, Career, and the Conflict of Modern Motherhood.

What's Lost: Friendship Breakups and Losses

The Final Picture

SAMANTHA BRINN MEREL

Seeing the final picture was a punch to the gut, apparently one more than I could endure.

I saw it on Facebook last night as I was mindlessly perusing the pictures of new babies and end-of-summer vacations, and about fifty links to the YouTube video of a Jewish singing group singing a popular Hebrew song to the tune of Anna Kendrick's "Cups."

I knew that she was getting married this past Sunday. All day, as I enjoyed the last hours of my Jersey Shore family vacation, people I knew were posting pictures of the festivities. I could almost follow the events in real time as I refreshed my Facebook feed.

She got her nails done. Got dressed. Took pictures. Walked down the aisle. Stood under a chuppah and married her man. Danced the afternoon away.

And I wasn't there, because she didn't want me to be there.

Every time a new picture was posted on Sunday, it was more evidence that what we had was no longer. Every time I saw the smiling faces of people I have known for twelve years – many of whom remain my closest friends today – my stomach jumped, but didn't settle.

I was in a free-fall, never quite knowing when I would hit the ground.

Day became night and the pictures slowed as the afternoon wedding came to an end. I went to sleep, still reeling from the constant barrage of documentary proof of the end of a friendship that I had always assumed would last forever. And I woke up yesterday morning resigned to the fact that Sunday was just substantiation of what I had really already known.

And then last night I saw the final picture.

A semi-darkened ballroom. All of my college friends huddled together, arms around each other. Her in the center, smile beaming, wedding dress glowing.

Maybe it was seeing everyone together that got to me, but I found myself staring at the picture, looking for an empty space that I would have filled. Wondering if anyone was thinking about me. Wondering if she was.

Tears pricked my eyes as the loneliness that had been hovering since Sunday came crashing in. I laid down on my bed and let them flow. I cried for myself, for her, and for the girls we used to be before everything changed. I cried for the whole life that I will have that she won't be a part of. I cried for the new husband she has that I have never met, and for the kids I hope to have that she will never know. I cried for a friendship that was once full of promise and fun. I cried because that's what I do when the hurt is too deep for words.

And when I finally cried myself dry I sat up and I understood. All the complexity had been washed away and I was left with only this.

I miss my friend.

Samantha Brinn Merel is a lawyer, runner, writer and pop-culture junkie living in the suburbs of New York City. She drags herself out of bed to run at dawn, writes blog posts on her iPad during her morning commute to Manhattan, and spends her nights in front of the TV with her equally television-addicted husband. She was selected as a top-13 finalist of Blogger Idol 2013 and blogs at This Heart of Mine.

My Grief Twin

JESSICA SMOCK

When someone you love becomes terminally ill, a lot of people respond by talking about it all the time. They can't stop sharing details about their loved one, their illness, the experience of death, and grief. Others turn inward and process their emotions by thinking about and talking about anything else. They share small moments here and there of their private grief, but for the most part, they keep their experience walled off from their relationships with other people.

When my dad became sick with lung cancer and died several months later, I closed myself off from most people. What I was experiencing was too big, too intense, to share with strangers, or even casual colleagues, those with whom I could not trust my heart. I couldn't risk talking about this with anyone whose trust was not as certain and as solid as rock.

But for my closest friends and those whom I trusted most, I clung to them like a drowning swimmer clutching onto to a life raft. I needed their words of comfort and reassurance more than I needed air, sleep, water, or food. In normal times I craved solitude outside of my normal routines of work, exercise, and friendships. Now I craved constant companionship and conversation. I thought that if I talked about it enough – my dad's sickness, my own grief, death and mortality – that I would suddenly understand its finality and its implications for my life and for my mom, sister, and brother. My closest friends listened – God, they listened — sat with me, took my phone calls at all hours. But there were truly no words that could mitigate the pain or that could make any rational sense of watching someone so young get so sick.

And then I started talking to Christina.

Another friend told me that she had a close friend, a former colleague that I had never met, who was going through what sounded like the same experience that I was. She was the same age, had a dad in his early fifties (like my dad) who was in the end stages of cancer, and she was also a teacher. My friend mentioned Christina several times and said that I should contact her, but I couldn't imagine calling up a stranger out of the blue and saying, "Hey, my dad has cancer too!"

However, after my dad passed away a few weeks later and I returned to Boston, I kept thinking of this girl. It turns out that her dad had died a couple weeks before mine. And then our mutual friend mentioned that Christina was going through a breakup with her boyfriend, just as I was, at the same time as dealing with her dad's death. (I was living with a boyfriend at the time, who had chosen to move out and announce the end of our relationship at the same time as my dad's death.) Who was this person who was living my parallel life? Was she dealing with it better? Maybe she had the answers that could ease my pain, comfort me more than those who could not possibly understand.

So I called her. And it was like a window into my own soul. We talked for hours, everything about our dads, cancer, stupid men who break our hearts, worries about our mothers and siblings. I knew nothing else about her. All the other reasons for forming a friendship – having common interests, a similar personality, shared background – had no bearing. All that mattered was this huge impossible task of learning how to mourn. We didn't talk about television shows, hobbies, clothes, our work days. Her friendship felt like having a terrible, rare disease and then finding a medical specialist who knew everything about your condition.

And then as months passed, I spent more time with my old friends and alone. I dated again. The mundane aspects of friendship – seeing a movie, dissecting an old friend's stupid career move – mattered again. Christina and I called each other less and less until we didn't speak at all.

But sometimes I wonder about this girl, my twin in grief. I don't know where she is and honestly can't remember her last name. But I hope she is well and has found joy and meaning from her life and knows that her friendship helped me to survive the hardest moment of my life.

Jessica Smock is a writer, educator, former teacher, researcher, and mom to a toddler son. She earned her doctorate in education from Boston University last spring and graduated from Wesleyan University. She writes about parenting, education, and books at her blog School of Smock *and at the* Huffington Post.

Stronger Than Me

ROSE TOWNSEND

I hate being sick. It makes me miserable and angry. (Ask my husband.) I resent the time lost and dwell on tasks undone. I curse my body for betraying me. For preventing me from operating at full capacity. I don't have time for that shit.

Fortunately (for everyone), it doesn't happen often. Recently, I got sick for the first time in years. I reacted exactly as described above. While I complained and whined and cursed the nasty virus, I thought about my college roommate.

I thought about the night I met her. I pictured her sitting in the house we shared as I unpacked. Arms wrapped around her knees, talking and listening. The conversation came easily and we were instant friends.

I thought about sitting across from her at dinner. We made "real" meals together. Actual chicken (shake and bake) and veggies (frozen) and noodles (from a box). Pretty classy by college standards. She would sit and say, "Mmm mmm," as we bragged about our gourmet meal to our housemates. (They were so freaking jealous.)

I thought about playing beer pong in our basement and drinking shots of rum and grape Kool-Aid. And dancing. Crazy, dizzy dancing that involved loud singing and jumping and smiling until our faces hurt.

I thought about lazy weekends. I pictured her on the couch watching cheesy Lifetime movies and eating take out.

I thought about watching the only girl fight I have ever seen, which may or may not have involved her kicking someone's ass while I watched in shock and admiration.

I thought about her dancing at my wedding. And about how happy I was to meet her fiancé and be at her wedding shower. And how amazing they both were with my kids a year later when met for a winter walk at a park.

I thought about the phone call I got a few weeks later. The news shook me, but her voice never wavered. Breast cancer, she said. *This isn't going to kill me*, she said. *I just have to get through it*. No tears. No nonsense.

I thought about the timeline. Done by next year at this time. Back on track with her life's plan. One year later arrived and all was well. I admired her strength and courage and ability to remain calm and focused. She did it. I knew she would.

I thought about the phone call a few months later. The cancer was back. In her lungs and inoperable. She talked casually about leg surgery and being unable to climb the stairs in her house. She was in her early thirties. I felt angry. I'm sure she must have too, but she never said it to me. She kept me up to date on her condition and asked what was going on in my life.

I thought about her concern for her husband. About how she joked over lunch that if anything happened to her, he wouldn't know how to access their bank accounts. She would give him a tutorial just in case. She talked about him often. She thought about what he needed. About how he was suffering. So completely selfless. So very in love.

I thought about the last time I saw her. My five-year-old saw a money jar in her living room and forwardly asked if he could borrow some. She quickly grabbed her wallet and made his day by giving him some change. She had made so many of my days just by being there.

I thought about one of our last conversations. The cancer was in her brain. She talked about her weekend away with her husband and time at the beach with family. She talked about how there were still more medications to try. The doctor said they would keep trying. If she knew she was close to the end, she never let on to me. Still no tears, no complaints. Just unbelievable courage.

I thought about the voice mail I left her the day before she died. I thought about the snow on the way to her funeral. I thought about how there is no way that all she was could fit into the tiny box they wheeled up the aisle of the church that morning.

I thought about her strength. Since the day I met her, she personified strength. I admired her for it then. I am in awe of it now. I don't know how the hell she fought the fight she did. I was pissed at a virus that would be over in a few days. She had been fighting for her life. But she was much stronger than me.

I would like to say that all these thoughts made me stop being a miserable sick person, that I sucked it up and showed a little of the strength I saw in her. But that would be a lie.

What these thoughts did do, was make me even more thankful to have known her. Thankful that someone that kind, that honest, that fun, that strong would call me a friend. Thankful to have spent a year under the same roof–laughing, crying, singing, dancing and really living with her. Thankful that we kept in touch. Thankful to have told her she was one of my all time favorite people (she totally was). Thankful she met my children. Thankful for that last hug and that I can still remember the sound of her voice so clearly. And see her smile. And picture her dancing.

As for getting angry at illnesses and life's other annoyances, I'm guessing she would advise me to be strong and positive. She would probably tell me not to be so miserable. She would encourage me to embrace every moment I have here whether those moments are ideal or painful. I'm pretty sure she wouldn't want me to complain or feel sorry for myself. As her passing tragically proved, we don't have time for that shit.

Rose Townsend is a stay at home mom with three children and a leader of her local Down syndrome interest group. She has a degree in Elementary Education and a passion for music. She blogs about using her children's interests, nature, music and travel to create meaningful learning experiences for the whole family at Naturally Educated.

How Motherhood Changes Friendship

Dani Ryan

Sally and I met during my last year of college, and developed a friendship that could withstand anything.

Boyfriends, break-ups, girls' weekends, PMS, marriages, new homes, my miscarriage, her divorce...

You name it, we did it.

Together.

But then I got pregnant and, unbeknownst to me, I broke the rules of our friendship.

Possibly forever.

I'd often heard that motherhood causes friendships to change, but I was naïve enough to think Sally and I could get through anything. I figured if I could clean her puke off the walls of a public restroom after one too many Jäger bombs on a Friday night, she could handle the sight of my bleeding, cracked nipples when she came to visit me after my daughter was born.

But I was wrong.

The year after my daughter's birth was filled with a myriad of disappointments when it came to Sally. I knew in my heart it was hard for her to watch me go through all of the things she so desperately wanted for herself, and that she probably didn't mean to hurt me when she started to pull away from me, but it's hard to keep that kind of perspective when you're a blubbering mess of postpartum hormones.

Of course, I've never been comfortable with confrontation, especially with those I love, so rather than being upfront and honest with her, I kept my feelings to myself. Well, that's not entirely true. I may have kept my feelings from her, but I certainly didn't keep them from my husband.

For better or for worse, right?

Months later, when I'd pulled myself out of my postpartum funk and finally come to terms with the fact that my friendship with Sally was coming to an end, she called me out of the blue to tell me she was (very unexpectedly) pregnant, and in the weeks that followed, she made it clear she wanted to be my BFF again. The only problem is, I didn't feel the same way. It just didn't feel genuine, and I needed time to process it all.

As her pregnancy progressed, we continued to keep in touch, but we both knew things weren't the same between us. And then, about a month before her due date, she went completely silent on me, and any attempt I made to contact her to see how things were going was met with complete and utter silence.

I initially took this as a sign that she was angry with me, but when three months went by without so much as a text message to let me know she'd had her baby, I started to get really worried.

Why didn't she contact me after her son was born?

Had something bad happened?

Should I keep trying to contact her, or was I just making things worse?

I agonized over those questions for weeks, and then one afternoon I decided to send her one last e-mail to tell her I was thinking of her, and that I would not be reaching out to her again.

A week later, she finally responded to that e-mail, and do you know what she said to me? She said she had been too busy and overwhelmed to find the two minutes it would've taken her to send me a text to tell me she was okay.

And she seemed keen on the idea of becoming BFFs again.

My initial reaction was to tell her to take her friendship and shove it, but motherhood has softened me, and I felt like I owed it to Sally and me to at least try. I know things will never be the same between us, but good friends are hard to come by, and there was a time when Sally was a good friend to me.

And I to her.

So I put on my big girl underpants and sent her a long, overdue email explaining how I'd been feeling. I figured if we had any chance of rekindling our friendship, we needed to be honest with each other.

It's been a month since I sent that e-mail, and I still haven't had a response. And you know what? I'm okay with that. It may not be the ending I had hoped for when I opened up about my feelings and tried to fix things with Sally, but at least I know I tried.

It's always sad to say goodbye to friendships, especially the ones that are marked with the craziness that takes place when you're a twentysomething trying to figure out where you belong in the world. But I'm not the same person I was at 24. And neither is Sally.

In my heart, I know my friendship with Sally isn't over. We'll find our way back to each other again one day. I'm sure of it.

And until that day arrives, I wish her the best of luck.

Sore nipples and all.

Dani Ryan is a SAHM who likes to make people laugh by sharing funny stories about her functionally dysfunctional life, both before and after she became a parent. It keeps her from opening the wine at 9 am. Sometimes. Her humor blog, Cloudy, With a Chance of Wine, *was selected as one of the three 2013 Funny Blogs to Watch by* Circle of Moms, *and she was a contributing author to the best-selling anthology,* I Just Want to Pee Alone.

The Miles Between Us

Erica Heller

Mandy and I met just once before we became roommates. A mutual friend suggested we move in together since neither of us could afford a one-bedroom in the pricey college town to which we were both relocating. We secured a two- bedroom apartment online, left for separate summers, and arrived in town a week before our graduate classes began.

As a logic-driven, athletic, assertive person, I don't click with a lot of women – it seems they find me overly direct and not gentle enough. The first week Mandy and I circled each other gingerly, but began sharing strategies for the transition we were both making: directions to the DMV, where to find a cheap, tasty burrito. We quickly found that we made excellent roommates, and had many quirky similarities in our personal histories. As an engineer, Mandy also operates from a predominantly logical mind frame, so our communication was easy and natural. As we each began to get a few social invitations, we shared those, too. Finally, we tried running together, and found we were well matched in stride, pace and distance – eureka!

Before long, Mandy and I were nearly inseparable. We cooked dinner together most nights, had the same social circle, and developed a hundred inside jokes. We both settled in and got quite busy but we often made a point to schedule our run together. We giggled even as we huffed along, talked about being bridesmaids in each others' weddings, and eventually shared the most painful, raw parts of ourselves. I haven't had a friendship quite like it since middle school, full of shared discovery, with the intensity of a romance. If I were to repeat some of what she told me about herself, you might understand more of what happened later, but I won't, not ever. The sharing that happens when you're that intimate is sacred, even if the sanctuary crumbles.

Mandy met one of my mountaineering buddies, Ben. He's a warm, affectionate person who flirted casually with most women until the moment he met Mandy. Instantly, she was the sun and the moon to him. It only took a few weeks before she felt the same about him. I was thrilled; it was fun to be in the glow of their giddy love, and I was crazy about both of them, so I had no problem with the fact that he spent a huge amount of time at our place. But as we were about to finish our degrees, Mandy began to pull away. I asked her why, and eventually she let me know I'd transgressed an important boundary: I'd used her special nickname for Ben as if it were mine, too. I was taken aback, as we'd shared every little expression and gesture for two years, but it made perfect sense that they needed separateness in their relationship. I apologized, and never did it again, but she continued to treat me as a third wheel. It started to get annoying, but we all were under the pressure of finishing up, so I let it slide.

We all graduated, moved out, and I rambled around Asia for several months. I figured that when I got back, Mandy and Ben's relationship would have settled in, and she and I would continue being best friends without the co-habitation. After a fun initial reunion, I called every few days, but Mandy put me off saying how busy she was. I fell back to our old strategy: I offered to join her for a run, knowing she always made time for her daily workout. When that took weeks, I knew something was up. Once we were finally on the trail hitting a good stride, I asked her *what had I done? How could I fix it?*

Mandy said she just wasn't comfortable any more with how people had seen us as a unit. She referenced her typical pattern of keeping her close female friends in distinct social groups. She'd made some new friends through Ben and she didn't want me to meet them. But she assured me I hadn't done anything wrong for which I should – or could – make amends. It was basically the age-old, *It's not you, it's me.* She suggested we spend "less" time together. Since we'd previously had daily contact, that seemed easy to achieve within a healthy friendship. But after several months in which my regular invitations yielded two stilted visits and no reciprocation, I felt frustrated and hurt. I said, *It's too weird begging to be around you.* I was explicit: *I'll give you some space, I won't call you, but please, call me as soon as you're ready.* That was eleven years ago. She hasn't called.

Initially, when we saw each other at gatherings it was intensely painful for me, and more so that she seemed unaffected. I hoped for her call, but there was nothing for months until an invitation to her out-of-state wedding showed up in the mail. I had a rush of hope that she was also inviting me back into her life. I reached out cautiously by e-mail with something leading like, *I got the invitation, thank you! The venue sounds great, I'm curious to hear more about it. How are you?* Mandy replied, *I'm good but very busy. I hope you're doing well. It would be great if you can make it.* Ouch. I realized it was Ben who wanted to include me. Still, I waited until the day of the deadline before I checked "Regretfully Declines" on the RSVP.

I may have burned a bridge by not going, but I'm pretty sure it was already destroyed. Seriously, would it have made sense to travel all that way to stand wistfully watching Mandy in a crowd of people, while knowing that she had no intention of seeing me in the town where we both lived? I had a final cry-myself-to-sleep over it during the weekend of her wedding, and then resolved to make my peace with our distance.

After a couple of years, I could see her without getting a lump in my throat. When I ran into her a week before the birth of her first child, I knew what to say to make her feel ok, and she thanked me, and it felt good to be able to do something small but positive with our old intimacy. The last time I saw Mandy was at a party when her daughter was a few months old. I toted the baby around for a while, giving Mandy and Ben a chance to mingle. Our interactions felt lighthearted, if superficial. I felt healed.

I had my first child, a son, several years later. My husband and I chose a classic but uncommon name, Miles, as a tribute to his paternal grandmother, Millie. Miles was not an easy baby, but he's the apple of my eye. When Miles was about five months old, a friend called to gently tell me some news: *Mandy and Ben just had their baby boy. And, well, I thought you should know... they named him Miles.* When our surprised mutual friend asked if she'd heard the news and name of my son, Mandy reportedly said vaguely, *Hmm, yeah, I think I did hear that.*

I was amazed that the anger and grief I thought was gone came rushing back that day, and stayed with me for several months whenever I thought about it. For me, Mandy's choice of a name for her son encapsulated everything about her and me: how much we're alike, how far she pushed us apart, and how completely she shed any feeling of connection to me. That quirky little sameness in our mothering further hints at another layer of loss; of what we might have been to each other as support through the challenges of transitioning from our efficient, active pre-child selves into the milky, sleep-deprived terrain of motherhood. Then again, had we stayed friends, only one of us could have used the name, since it would have been too darn confusing when we called out to our two little boys scampering together up the trail...

As it is, despite my strong initial reaction, Mandy is right: the fact that our sons have the same name simply doesn't matter. It's been nearly four years since her son was born, and we've never even met each other's Miles.

Erica Heller is the lucky and exhausted mom of two preschoolers and wife of an amazing husband and father. She has published professionally as an urban planning consultant but has never penned a personal blog before. She was greatly honored as the subject of an essay Stephanie Sprenger wrote to kick off HerStories.

Best Friends

Dresden Shumaker

It happens every couple of years. You lose a best friend. Or you realize that you have a bad friend. Or you laugh at the phrase, "best friends forever."

Sometimes the end of a friendship happens out of the blue – like that moment when you can't find your keys and you *know* you just had them. Sometimes it happens like the dress at the back of your closet – you had forgotten how much you loved it and decide to wear it again or you realize it no longer fits and you really should let it go.

I am amazed by people who have had best friend relationships for decades and decades. In my lifetime I have had at least 17 best friends. I have had moments of my life where I had no one I would claim as a bestie, and some moments (like now, for instance), where I am lucky enough to have several best friends.

Yes, I do believe it is possible to have more than one best friend. And, yes, I do know that by doing so, the term "best" doesn't really fit, but I have a team of best friends and it is fantastic. I also recognize that for every different life I have lived, I have needed someone (or a team of someones) to help me through.

But then there is that moment. That moment when the person that is at the top of your speed dial stops calling you. That moment when you realize you have stopped calling them. There is that moment when you go through something huge and the person you had thought was your best friend is nowhere to be found. There is that moment when you realize you were not invited. There is that moment when you watch their life pass you by on platforms like Facebook and there is a hurt there. A specific hurt.

I have no idea whatever happened to best friends 2, 3, 4, 5, 6, 10 and 13. I reconnected with 1, my first best friend (yup, from first grade!), when I was in my late 20's. We had an intense and powerful catchup and marveled at the common threads of our lives. We even met up and I introduced best friend 1 to best friend 11 (they lived in the same town!) and I watched, from afar, as they became friends and then watched as the friendship faded away. As they often do.

Friends 7, 8, 9, 12, and 14 have evolved to being friends online. I have stood on the sidelines and watched them fall in love, move to new states, get married, have children... There are some where I pause and think, "I used to know everything about you. We used to talk. Now we don't." Now I am an FBFF (former best friend forever) and relegated to liking the photo from their wedding day or saying "Congrats!" when they announce the birth of their son.

There is an acceptance of, a normalcy even, when we lose a school friend as we move forward with life. It is incredibly rare to find someone who is still best friends with the person that they were best friends with from elementary school, high school, heck, even college. So when those friendships fade away, we let them. We celebrate the wonderful, powerful, meaningful moments that we had and then cast the friendship out to sea so that another person can pick it up.

What is most painful are the best friend relationships lost as an adult. Things happen. Big things. Small things. Maybe they got married. Maybe you had a kid. Maybe you moved away. Maybe politics evolved. Maybe you have no idea what happened. You just woke up one morning realizing the shift had happened.

I know many women that have endured a best friend loss as an adult. It is truly horrible to go through. It can even be messy and awkward as we cling to old familiars and try to repair something that has disintegrated. Sometimes we just have to let go. In our hearts we know this. In actuality it is devastating.

It is personal evolution, and we all go through it. The hard moment when you realize your best friend didn't invite you to something is a gift. The moment when your best friend says something wildly offensive or mean – that is a favor to you. The moment when you realize that your best friend never calls you – that is your answer.

Walk away. Slip away. Release it.

As gut-crushing as it is to move away from a friendship, it is a million times more wonderful to realize that the person or people that you *do* have are amazing. There *were* people there for you when you were going through that awful thing. There were people there congratulating you on that victory. There was someone for you to call to yell, "OMG! Turn on your TV!"

Thank you to the best friends that I have had: past, present, and future.

Dresden Shumaker chronicles her adventures in single parenting on CreatingMotherhood.com. *For the last few years she has worked in new media for a tech startup in Philadelphia, as a web designer, as a graphic artist, and as a freelance writer. She covers entertainment news for* Babble.com *and is a contributor to* Kids in the House. *Dresden's writing has been featured or syndicated in* The Huffington Post, The Good Men Project, AimingLow, Parenting, Type-A Parent, *and* BlogHer.

A Friendship Mourned

DANA HEMELT

Some women meet their forever friends when they are little girls, running on the playground and trading snacks in the cafeteria. Some meet them in middle and high school, sharing secrets, clothes, and dreams. While I had friends during those years, it wasn't until I went to college that I met the first of my forever friends.

Allysa and I met on the day we moved into the dorms our freshman year, and we lived together for four years. We grew from girls to young women alongside one another, and my friendships with Allysa and my four other roommates were as precious to me as my education. In fact, these friendships *were* an education; these were the years when I was figuring out who I was, and the six of us relied on one another to navigate our way into the grown-up world.

I didn't have close friends in high school, so Allysa was one of my first true girlfriends. She and my other roommates were the only people I lived with who were not my family. But she became my family, and Allysa was the friend with whom I planned my future. We often took long walks in the neighborhood surrounding our campus, talking about our lives after college. We imagined what our marriages would be like, which careers we would choose, and how our homes would be decorated. We talked about our future children, deciding on the perfect birth order/ gender split as if we had the power to make it happen. I wanted a boy first and then a girl, and Allysa thought she might prefer to only have boys. There were so many possibilities, and we loved dreaming about what our lives would be like when we graduated.

College ended, but the six of us made good on our pact of keeping in touch. While we were no longer involved in each other lives on a daily basis, the friendships endured. Some of us started graduate school, and some of us started jobs. We kept in touch with regular telephone chats, and we made the four hour car trip for weekend visits a few times a year.

Two years after graduation, Allysa was a bridesmaid in my May wedding, and we all celebrated another roommate's wedding in July. Two of us drove up to spend the weekend with her in November. A little over a month later, my phone rang in the early morning hours on New Year's Day. I watched my husband as he answered the call, and I knew the voice on the other end was delivering horrible news even before I heard it myself. My dear friend had taken her own life. Allysa was 24 years old.

The loss was devastating, made bearable only by the support of my new husband and the four other women who were reeling from the same tragedy. I avoid revisiting those first few months of grief. I feel that focusing on the details of Allysa's death and its aftermath would overshadow what I choose to remember: a big-hearted, loyal and bright young woman whose friendship was an integral part of my life.

When my daughter was born (how I wished I could tell Allysa that having a girl first was just fine), I experienced the loss in a fresh way. My friend would never know my kids, and the world was denied the wonderful children I know Allysa would have raised. I mourned my friend all over again, and I grieved for her parents with a rawness that I didn't know existed before I was a mother myself.

Allysa has been gone for almost eighteen years. She has been missing from my life for so many more years than she was in it.

I don't think about her every day, but I will remember her at unexpected times and a memory will make me smile. A song that she always sung with the wrong lyrics, her favorite color purple, a funny abbreviation she made up for a phrase or word. The friends that are in my life now — my other four roommates, the women I've met since becoming a mother — they are all so important to me, but they are friends of the person that I am now. Allysa was the friend of a different Dana, and I wonder how our friendship would have changed as time and life changed us.

Allysa will always be young, and my friendship with her will always be one of two young women at the beginning of their life story. When I remember Allysa, I also remember the girl that I was — the girls we both were — sharing our dreams and planning our lives full of promise. Our friendship reminds me that this young woman, the one with all those plans and dreams, is still a part of who I am today.

My life isn't exactly as we planned it, Allysa, but it's pretty darn good. How I wish you were here to share it with me.

Dana Hemelt is using her Master's degree in Clinical Psychology to stay at home and raise two brilliant and well adjusted children. She's the next great novelist, stand-up comic, fashionista, and interior decorator all trapped in the body and life of a suburban mom. And least that's how she's sees it in her head. You can find her writing about a little bit of everything at her blog, Kiss my List.

Baby Showers and Silver Linings

STEPHANIE SPRENGER

I had always longed to have a pregnancy friend. I pictured us sitting side by side on the couch, our swollen feet propped up, passing the Ben and Jerry's back and forth, and swapping bladder problem stories. We would most definitely pose for the requisite belly-to-belly photograph, and our children would undoubtedly grow up to be best friends. When I had my first daughter, I was the first of my close friends to get pregnant, and thus was left without a belly buddy. I had high hopes that I would find another mom friend who was expecting when I began trying to conceive a second child, but things weren't looking promising.

In early September, the week before I was to attend a friend's baby shower, I took a pregnancy test. It came back positive, and I floated through the festivities the day of the party with a combination of smugness at my secret and the sensation that I was bursting with the desire to share my news. My first daughter was four years old, and I had experienced miscarriage prior to her conception, so I was mindful to keep the exciting news to myself for as long as I could. As it turns out, *as long as I could* wasn't very long at all.

Erica, a woman I knew just slightly through our mutual friend, was also at the party. When she shyly declined the offer of a mimosa, I exchanged a knowing glance with her. She confessed that she was six weeks pregnant, and unable to contain myself at this news, I blurted out that I was five weeks along. Interestingly, when reminiscing about this party years later, Erica's recollection was a bit different. She remembered that *I* was the one who spilled the beans first! Memory is a funny thing, isn't it? *Maybe I will*

217

have a pregnancy friend, I thought excitedly, getting ahead of myself. The two of us babbled excitedly with a mixture of neuroses and enthusiasm, promising to get in touch after the shower.

About a week later I received an email from Erica. The subject line read simply ":(" and I knew immediately what had happened. She wrote, *Hey, FYI: I had a miscarriage yesterday at seven weeks. I hope things are going better for you!*

I started bleeding the next day. The subsequent weeks were a frenzy of emails as we offered support, advice, and an opportunity to vent to one another. I found that I had little interest in interacting with anyone other than Erica. Only she truly understood what I was going through. I knew my other friends cared for me and had the best of intentions, but even the ones who had previously experienced loss weren't experiencing it right at that instant. Erica and I could tell each other everything, from our feelings of bitterness and frustration to our intense desire to begin trying to conceive again as soon as possible. During those tumultuous first weeks after my pregnancy loss, I found that I had unconsciously begun to cocoon myself; I couldn't stand to be around anyone who might unintentionally look at me as though they felt sorry for me. My emotions felt wildly irrational, as did my desire to avoid pregnant women and mothers with babies, and Erica became the one person I allowed inside my protective shell.

We shared meals, coffee, and wine as we wryly discussed our obsessive fertility charting and our half-hearted attempts to pretend we were approaching our next pregnancies with a laid-back, Zen attitude. It was safe to cry with her, but more likely than not we sat in the back booth of restaurants shaking the table with our raucous laughter. Waitresses walked by us smiling as we bellowed details of our personal lives that were not frequently shared in public.

Erica and I both got pregnant again, and our daughters are about two months apart. We of course attended one another's baby showers — both casual backyard affairs — in the stifling heat of summer. I made frequent trips to the bathroom at hers to confirm that I was not, in fact, leaking amniotic fluid, but was merely sweating copiously in my maternity sundress. Several days after her shower, it dawned on us that we had missed the perfect opportunity for that belly-to-belly photograph.

Oh, well. Erica, somewhat frantic, arrived late to my own baby shower, having left her newborn daughter at home for the first time, lamenting the fact that she had wasted half of her 90 minutes of freedom driving around lost thanks to her navigation system's failure to locate my new house. We took several morning walks in the last few weeks of my pregnancy, me waddling uncomfortably as she soothed her newborn, tucked in a front carrier.

In the three years since she became my confidante, I continue to turn to Erica with situations that I feel uncomfortable discussing with others. We are a sounding board for each other when struggling with parenting issues, marital challenges, or personal fulfillment. Though there are times when one of us calls in tears, the hysterical laughter has become a cornerstone of our friendship. Erica is one of the funniest people I know, and no subject is off limits for her self-deprecating commentary. I will laugh until my sides hurt as she describes her awkward moments of pumping breastmilk in her office, and I know she will appreciate the story of my daughter making up song lyrics about the anatomical terminology she learned for her private parts.

We possess an emotional intimacy that I treasure, and our shared pregnancy loss was only the beginning of our connection. If one must find a silver lining amidst suffering, I claim my friendship with Erica as one of the most beautiful things to come out of a time of grief.

Stephanie Sprenger is a freelance writer, music therapist, and mother of two young daughters. She writes about the imperfect reality of life with kids on her blog, Mommy, for Real. *Her work has been featured on various websites, including* Mamalode, In the Powder Room, BlogHer, *and* Scary Mommy. *Stephanie was a cast member of the Denver production of Listen To Your Mother in May 2013.*

The Friend Breakup

ANNE-MARIE LINDSEY

I thought that I was a fearless blogger, because I write about motherhood, mental health and psychiatric medication, until a speaker at a conference asked us if there were stories that we were afraid to tell, stories that made us uncomfortable. (Not me!) She urged us to write them, because readers needed to know that someone else had been through it, too, whatever it was. (I do that!) She held back tears as she explained that she had recently been through a "friend breakup," but she couldn't find anything to read on the subject. (Oh...)

All the while I had been blogging, I had also relied on an online network of friends for support, but it had never occurred to me to write about friendship on a blog. Again: I blog about motherhood. Who are you going to talk to, besides blogging strangers, about pregnancy, birth, motherhood and antidepressants, if not a close friend? Why had I left friendship off my list of helpful resources?

The short answer: because it's not always such a helpful resource. Friendship is amazing, when it clicks, and friends come through. I share an incredible bond with a friend who gave birth to her first child just a few months before I had mine, because we shared conception, pregnancy, birth and "OMG! I have a kid!" stories all along the way. When friends fall silent or disappear, especially at times of great need, however, our hearts break.

I want to feel surprise, but don't, when I consider how few "My Friend Broke My Heart" stories are out there, even in a Blog Everything world. This part of female friendship is rarely discussed, although society seems to revel in the fact that women often love their "best friends" so passionately. "BFF" and "bestie" have become part of the vernacular, but there are no words for the end of these relationships. *Sex and the City* had reached its peak popularity by the time I was in college, and groups of women friends huddled close, sharing secrets, were idealized by the women at my school, with our new-found freedom and, despite attending a women's college, proximity to the boys "across the street." There were plenty of "whatabitch" stories about acquaintances. But no one mentioned the pain of childhood friendships that fizzled out when the friends chose colleges on opposite coasts. In an environment where every breakup was dissected and pulled apart, friendships that ended badly seemed shrouded in silence. There was pressure to smile and make small talk. Be nice. Share friends without making a fuss.

I went through more than one strange, painful friend breakup, but enough time has passed to give me the distance and perspective I need to write the story of my most painful broken heart. I wouldn't have picked Lucy out to be the heart-breaking type, when our friendship began. She lived down the hall from me, and when I asked about her singing, which I had heard her practice, she helped me find a voice teacher. We cheered each other on at auditions for the fall musical, and neither of us got parts. We thought it was so cool when we found her in the background in one of my photos from move-in day. My dad and I are standing at the gates, and there she is, walking out the gates, right behind me.

Somehow, she made friends with the cheerleader who lived at the end of the hall, while I made friends with a girl from my poetry class, and the four of us came together sometime during that first winter at school. The four of us had fun. Lucy was good at talking us into stuff, like the First-Years' Ball. Why get all dressed up and go to a dance at a university with a 3:1 girl:boy ratio? I have no memory of any actual argument in favor of going, but I think it was just the sheer force of Lucy's will that got us to go. We even had an okay time, somehow, despite disappointing food and, as we predicted, not a cute (or straight) boy in sight. There are some great pictures of all of us giggling.

Part of what attracted the four of us to each other at the time was that we all needed financial aid at a very expensive college and, as we would learn much later, we all needed therapy for anxiety and depression.

Relative poverty and depression don't seem like attractive traits, of course, but they gave us something to overcome that most of our classmates did not experience. While financial aid was a relatively rare experience at our school, therapy was hardly uncommon. What we shared, it turned out, was a genetic mental health handicap. Our burdens became, in turn, too heavy, and each of us needed help. Given the nature of those struggles combined with other, more ordinary, transformations, the group dynamic was bound to change, as we became more aware of the changes happening in our lives, individually.

The first test came during the incredibly stressful hunt for sophomore housing; three of us would be living together, but Lucy would not be invited. She had said that she wanted to live with friends, because she needed people to "take care of me." It's hard for me to separate what her behavior was like before she was diagnosed with a serious mental illness and medicated — and this was nine years ago. I don't remember what it was, exactly, that needed taking care of. I do remember that none of us wanted to be responsible for taking care of a roommate. That was a separation she had not anticipated, and I don't remember hearing her air her feelings about it. It may have been good preparation for all of us, though, given that we would be separated from the group we relied on and our individual friendships, in some pretty bizarre ways.

One friend abruptly dropped out of school, after confirming that her erratic behavior had been the result of both alcoholism and depression. Although this turned out to be temporary, and she eventually graduated, for the time being, she announced that she was moving to Spain to be an au pair. This was now junior year, however, the time almost half our class would use to study abroad, so I was right behind her. I lived in Edinburgh, Scotland, for a year. In January, our third friend moved to Prague. Why did Lucy stay? I don't remember. I think that her GPA had dropped too low, but it could also have been about money. The fact that I don't remember seems like an indication that I was not paying close attention. I wonder, now, if that hurt her.

I became closer to our au pair friend, after the family she worked for turned out to be insane, and she had to move in with me, in Scotland, until the agency could get her paid. I visited Prague and unexpectedly bonded with our friend there, when my persistent questions finally wore her down, and she admitted to a sexual experience that had left her upset, confused and ashamed. I was been there for our friends in ways that Lucy couldn't be; she was both far away and spiraling downward. By the time I returned from Scotland, she had been diagnosed with bipolar disorder but only intermittently complying with the treatment prescribed to her. This was dangerous, given that her prescription was lithium, a drug that can wreck you, physically, if you don't eat properly, drink enough water and take it on time. She was also struggling with her weight and fighting with her family, who lived nearby.

As Lucy became less reliable and her behavior more dangerous, I became increasingly withdrawn and depressed. I had made new friends and left them behind, but many of my New York friends were gone for the summer. My relationship with my father had become strained. Lucy was one of the few friends who was also living in the dorms for the summer. Looking back, I see so much in common, in our struggle to stay above water. We didn't see it, then. Instead of leaning on each other, we broke our friendship.

I still feel incredible guilt about the fact that I don't know what I did to upset Lucy. I must have done something. One day, I got a slip in my mailbox indicating that I had a package. As it turned out, I had many packages. The cardboard boxes contained everything that Lucy had ever borrowed from me. I was stunned. It still seemed possible that we could save the friendship, because we still had two close friends in common, but we didn't connect. She was clearly avoiding me. I was working three jobs, seven days a week. Why did we let something come between us, after such a long friendship? Why don't I know what it was, exactly, that did come between us? We were both struggling with our own mental health issues as well as difficult relationships with our parents. We were both lonely, living in nearly empty dorms, working during the summer, while many of our classmates enjoyed vacations or summer programs. I remember calling, and I remember that she didn't return my calls. Depression, and probably also the unbearable heat in my dorm room, make that whole summer a bit of a blur.

One night defines that summer, for me, and it will probably remain etched in my memory as long as I live. I went out on the fire escape outside my dorm room window in an attempt to escape the heat; it seemed romantic, especially because I could see a slice of the Hudson River just to the left of the building down the block. It was early evening. A noise below me caught my attention, and I looked down maybe ten stories at the men working below, moving heavy boxes and crates. (Only in New York City can you find a dorm above a Chinese restaurant.) The moment I looked down, the ground was suddenly so close and just far enough. The railing on the fire escape was so easy to climb over. In that moment, I simultaneously sat there, watching the boxes and crates, the tops of heads, the tiny arms, and I climbed over the railing and just... let go. It happened in my mind. And that put the fear of God into me.

Somehow, I got back through that window. I sat on my bed and called everyone who might possibly be able to come over. I was crying hysterically. No one picked up. I left messages. I don't know how long the list actually was, but it felt like I made 10,000 calls. I ended up talking to my mother, who was low on the list because she lives far away. Everyone called me back, eventually. Except Lucy. She never called to check on me. It hurt.

It. Hurt. So. Much.

I got myself into an intensive therapy program. After I had been deemed depressed enough to benefit from therapy twice a week, I began seeing a Columbia/Presbyterian hospital psychology fellow for free.

I don't remember how much interaction Lucy and I had over the next few months. The hurt in my heart festered. I didn't bring it up. She had sent my things back to me in boxes, through campus mail, when we were living just minutes from each other. When school started again, I didn't ask her why she hadn't called me back.

To this day, I have never heard Lucy's side to this story.

The months passed. My father got worse. I finished a senior thesis. I applied to thirteen graduate schools, each with a different deadline and different requirements; this meant, essentially, editing my thesis all over again, thirteen times. I was going to therapy twice a week, but I hadn't explored medication.

I remember a lot from that fall, but nothing concrete about Lucy. Have I blocked out interactions with her? Or, did they just not happen? At any rate, she sent out an e-mail to a long list of people, and it asked that we support her, because she was having a difficult time. The hurt that I had let fester in my heart exploded into rage. I had reached out to her, personally, by phone, and she hadn't even returned my call. That was probably around June. By December, she was including me in a group e-mail about her needs — I didn't trust myself to respond.

I never responded. I did mean to. December passed, including her Christmas birthday. January didn't bring me the words I needed. I stopped looking. As it turned out, I was spiraling down into a depression that would land me in the psych ward by spring break. The suicidal ideation that had prompted me to seek therapy was a walk in the park, compared to the night I spent actually planning how I might kill myself. The morning after that second, awful, night, I went straight to see my psychiatrist, who put me right into an emergency room and, from there, an inpatient program. I graduated on time, with honors, a feat I am still so proud to have accomplished.

But why didn't I ever write to Lucy?

Because I didn't want the friendship. It was heavy. It was hard. It was a relief to be free from it. My hurt over the phone call and the e-mail was my excuse. I felt manipulated. I felt like we had been locked in a competition, for years, over theater and music and talent, and I had never wanted to compete in the first place. I felt like we were in a competition over who our friends liked more. The friendship had begun to feel like something out of junior high, maintained so that we wouldn't rock the boat of The Group, for fear that one of us would be left out in the cold. I didn't respond to her email, because I didn't have the energy to support Lucy.

I never got in touch with Lucy again, because I didn't want to be asked to support her ever again. I'm sure that she has felt pain and rejection. I am the one who got to make a choice about that friendship.

We still have one friend in common, and it's still awkward. The last time I saw Lucy, we were both bridesmaids in our friend's wedding. We made conversation. It was fine. She met my husband; I met her boyfriend. That was the last time we saw each other. When I had a baby, she sent a card, through the same friend. When she got engaged, I sent a congratulatory message through LinkedIN (really). She got married. She lost the other friend we once shared after a fight about the wedding, and that friend asked to spend the weekend with me, instead of attending.

Their disagreements have nothing to do with me. But it is awkward that I saw this friend on a trip that was supposed to be for Lucy's wedding.

I am all right with the awkward, and I honestly hope that things stay where they are. The alternatives are, at best, bizarre and, at worst, petty. I don't want to stay angry. What would I do? Ask people not to mention her name? Pretend that I don't know that she got married, or that I didn't get the card for the baby? That idea is just weird and creepy.

I can't figure out why my heart still hurts, or why my feelings are still hurt. I call this a breakup, because that is what it is. Ex-boyfriends: I don't invite them over, but if pictures come across my newsfeed on Facebook, I click. Sometimes, I feel smug about my baby and my husband, if it looks like they're still single. It's less harsh with Lucy. I wish her joy, and with my whole heart. I do feel jealousy, when a friend is with her, and not me. Is that petty?

Breakups are messy and often petty. If there's actual love in a relationship, it never really goes away. The same is true of friendship. But it's hard to call for a girls' night out and a tear-fest when "the girls" are stuck in the middle and no one ever said the words, "It's over." The end of a romantic relationship has a script built into it. When a long friendship ends, all that's left are people in a mess with no script to follow and too much in common. There is nothing to say, except maybe, "This sucks."

Anne-Marie Lindsey is the author of the popular personal blog, Do Not Faint, *as well as the blog of the same name for* Psychology Today. *She also guest posts at parenting blog* Fit for Moms, The Fearless Formula Feeder, *and the* Feminist Breeder *Resource site. Anne-Marie's writing is driven by her desire to chronicle her journey through planning a pregnancy, pregnancy itself and, finally, motherhood, in the face of a life-long struggle with severe anxiety and depression. In addition to mothering and writing, she has recently added a third career; inspired by her own empowering birthing experience, she has begun working towards her certification as a HypnoBirthing® Instructor. Anne-Marie hopes to write a memoir to reach even more women who have struggled to advocate for themselves while facing mental health challenges.*

How I Became A Bad Friend

Kristi Rieger Campbell

During younger, more extroverted and needy years, I was a really good friend. While I admit that I've never been the type to remember to call any of you each and every day, just to check in, I've been the one who is always there. I've been the one that you likely called during a crisis. I'm the friend who leaves work at one in the afternoon after dashing out a quick excuse to my boss because I know that you need me.

I'm the friend who drives an hour and 15 minutes to travel 15 minutes away through a tornado warning, flooded roads, detours, and angry people, while bawling, with you, also bawling, on the phone, so that I can be there when it's time for you to say your last horrifying forever-goodbye to your dog. I am the friend who is there, even though we haven't spoken in weeks.

I'm the friend who has driven 11 hours to come and pick you up because you've admitted that the relationship I'd suspected was toxic and horrible actually is. I'm the one that encouraged you to sleep, after quickly packing your things, and driven us both 11 hours back to my home. Which became your home. No questions. I'm the friend who accepts, understands, and loves. I'm also the one who helps you to understand that your anger is justified and real, and am there to hold your hand while we both shed tears over the heartbreak of having to get a restraining order.

I'm the friend that you call when you want to leave your husband, and don't know who else to turn to. I'm the one that you trust to whisper the words that he's drained your bank account, and your soul, when you cannot tell your mother, because she lives with you. I'm the one that listens, because I want to. I am there, with you. I'm the friend who is there, even though I should be at work. I'm the one who works at ten p.m. to make up for our six-hour coffee talk.

To clarify, this has not been a one-sided friendship. You were there for me, during similar times, and worse ones, over and over again. You have been the one that I've called, at two a.m., panicked over ending a relationship. You're the one that I called when I got pregnant. Called when I was scared.

We have been good friends to one another. We are, or used to be, good and best friends.

We were good friends when I found out that my son has probably-autism, or something like it. You were a good friend when I first told you how frightened, and angry, and depressed I was. When we were able to talk about it. You were a good friend when you told me that he didn't seem that far behind.

When our play dates got harder. When you told me that it was okay. When I felt like I needed to apologize for my son.

But somewhere, during my son's lost words and lost exchanges, being friends became too hard on both of us. I know that we tried.

We tried. I thank you for inviting us to what you did, while you did. I thank you for coming to our invites, too. I thank you for trying to understand when I said that my son will not sit and eat cake with other kids. He will not sing the Happy Birthday song to your daughter. I mentioned it before we came, and you invited us, anyway. Thank you.

It's really the other people that messed up our friendship. And, sadly, the other people include our children. I feel horrible saying that. But when your kid cries because of mine? I'd rather be at home, alone with my son, playing with airplanes and dragons and water and bubbles. I'd rather wrap myself in my own world of it's-okay-ness. And I'd rather not hear your daughter wondering what's wrong with my son. I'd rather not hear you, telling me that it's fine.

Thank you for inviting us. I am so sorry that we left crying. I'm so sorry that we don't know how to play the same games that you enjoy with your kids. I'm sorry that we didn't fit in.

I'm more sorry that you don't want to try, any more. And, I'm even more sorry to say that neither do I.

I found new friends. Ones whose kids don't cry when my son is who he is. Which means that I don't cry when my son is who he is.

I still want to be your friend. But I can't hear what you're saying to me right now. And, in the meantime, I've found a friend who has a boy like mine. She and her son make it so that the pressure and the heart-squeeziness isn't there. I'm not anxious when I meet them for a play date. I'm not sad when my son's language sucks. I'm just there, and present, talking about things that you don't have to, or want to, talk about.

I don't hold the fact that you don't talk about them against you. I am happy for you with all that I am.

But, I'm also happy for me, with all that I am, that I've found a friend who understands what it means to have a little boy whose words are hard to understand. Whose actions don't make sense, in your world.

I'm grateful for my new friend.

But, I miss you. I miss you a lot.

Kristi Rieger Campbell is a semi-lapsed career woman with about eighteen years of marketing experience in a variety of national and global technology companies. More recently, she was a co-host on a hilarious (and under-funded) weekly radio show. Once her son was born, she became the mom who almost always leaves the house in either flip-flops or Uggs, depending on the weather. While she does work part-time, her passion is writing and drawing really stupid-looking pictures for her blog Finding Ninee. Finding Ninee *(pronounced nine-ee for her son's pronunciation of the word airplane) started due to a memoir, abandoned when Kristi read that a publisher would rather shave a cat than read another. Its primary focus is to find and provide humor and support in a "Middle World," one where the autism spectrum exists but a diagnosis does not.*

The Case For A Friendship Break

NINA BADZIN

Some former friends (okay, *most* former ones) are best left in the past. But sometimes an old friend can haunt you. She's the friend that got away. She's the one that's worth getting back.

I met Becky in August 1995 on the day we moved a few rooms apart in the same freshman dorm. I can still envision her standing at my door introducing herself. "I was *born* in Highland Park!" she said, referring to the cutesy door signs our resident advisors made about our hometowns.

Speaking more quickly than I did, which I had never thought possible, Becky explained that her parents moved her family from Highland Park (in Chicago) to Maryland. We marveled at the idea that we could have grown up together. *That* plus our instant chemistry lent a certain inevitability to our bond.

We claimed each other in that unspoken way that girls (and women) do when they become close quickly. We went to every party together. Ate every meal together. Obsessed about boyfriends together. We were each other's home base in those first months, then years, away from home.

Our rift didn't happen with a fight over a guy or something easy to name. An "incident" to reference would have been a comfort. No, instead our growing apart felt like a deep judgement on the people we were each trying to become.

It began slowly while Becky was abroad for a semester in Jerusalem and I was in Santiago. We came back for our senior year in different mindsets. I decided not to take the LSAT. I dropped my senior thesis (that I had spent eight months researching in Santiago). Within the first few months of our senior year, I met Bryan, whom I would end up marrying exactly two years later, so you can imagine that he had become a big focus of my time.

Becky had a serious boyfriend too, but she was going through her own strange year. We bickered a lot, doing a poor job of letting the other one grow and change. Becky would admit that she was harder on me than necessary that year. I can admit that I was a party-pooper, to put it mildly.

After college our long distance friendship felt forced, but since I didn't know how to let things drift to a natural end, I did something a bit dramatic. Essentially, I told Becky that I didn't think we should stay friends. My "wish" came true. We were not in each other's lives during my engagement or when I got married. I've been married for twelve years and I still can't believe Becky wasn't there. It doesn't seem possible considering how close we are now.

Author Julie Klam writes in her memoir *Friendkeeping*, "*There is something to be said for having 'breaks' in friendships. Sometimes you find there are things you need to do in your life and a certain friend may not support that change, at that moment anyway. It is very fair to allow people to grow and change, but it's nice to be able to come back home again, too.*"

After about two years, I missed Becky terribly. As Julie Klam put so well, I wanted to "come back home." I took a chance that she felt the same way and sent her a handwritten letter explaining how much our friendship had meant to me. I asked her to forgive me for not seeing a different way to handle my need for time apart years earlier.

Becky never wrote me back. I had set the terms for our break and now she had the right to determine if and when we would reconcile.

I think a year passed with no word from Becky, but when two of our mutual close friends had weddings planned for the same summer, there was no avoiding each other. During the first of those weekends we hugged (awkwardly) and decided to go for walk. By the end of that walk, our break was over. Becky addressed some of what I had written in the letter, but we honestly didn't harp on the past too much. We agreed (with ridiculous amounts of maturity) that however difficult and hurtful our "break" had been, it had served its purpose. We had ended up with time to grow into ourselves in ways that were hard for the other one to understand and therefore support.

Our original chemistry was back in full force and we found that we led similar lives with similar values. Bryan and I attended her wedding the next year. Our firstborn children (eight years old now) were born only months apart. We're now both moms of four and we've been there for each other (emotionally though not physically) after the births of each child in those first ugly months when everything makes you cry. We can go two months without talking then speak every day for a week as we try to get to the end of one simple story.

I feel Becky's college influence on my life even now. I had always admired how analytical Becky was, how bright, how proud of her Judaism. That I send my kids to a Jewish parochial school is directly connected to Becky. I wanted my children, like Becky, to move confidently and intelligently around all the details of our religion and culture, from the ins and outs of the Hebrew language to a deep knowledge and understanding of why we do what we do.

If that was all Becky had given me, it would have been enough. But she gave me so much more. She gave our friendship a second chance. For that and so much more she has my deepest respect, gratitude, and love.

Nina Badzin is a contributing writer for Brain, Child Magazine*'s blog and a freelance writer with work in a variety of websites and anthologies. She blogs at her personal site,* ninabadzin.com, *and lives in Minneapolis with her husband and four children.*

Afterword

We'd also like to add the story of our own friendship to the collection. It was Jessica who first approached Stephanie with the idea for a blog series about women's friendship; we had both recently read a fantastic book by Susanna Sonnenberg, *She Matters: A Life in Friendships,* and we felt inspired to somehow incorporate her exploration of female friendship into a series of essays. As the project evolved—from rotating blog posts to a brand new website to a rapidly growing anthology—a friendship began to evolve as well.

Our email correspondence, leaving a trail akin to old journal entries, chronicles the progression of our friendship from uncertain colleagues to unapologetic confidantes. The first several messages were filled with a blend of awkwardness and excitement:

From Jessica to Stephanie:

> I just finished the book you recommended, *She Matters,* about female friendships, and I absolutely loved it. I just think that it's such an unusual book; it's so rare that you encounter a unique take on the memoir. And I realized that this is EXACTLY how I go through my own life of memories — I don't remember events or times of my life based on my age or where I was living. I remember them based on my best friend at the time, and I think most women have that experience too, just like the writer does. I mentioned a while ago the idea of starting some kind of book club... I haven't forgotten about it.
>
> I've been thinking the past few days about an idea that I think I like, based on *She Matters*. And I'm hoping that you

think it's a good idea too and you might be interested! What about if we get another bunch of bloggers, writers, or regular people and start our own series on female friendships? Each piece would be a self- contained short essay about a writer's relationship with a friend from her life (sort of like the book, which is really more like a series of essays). We could feature writers — or just regular people — from all different age groups talking about their friendship experiences.

From Stephanie to Jessica:

I am so excited about this idea that I just read this email as fast as I can, so I need to go back and slowly digest the specifics of what you suggested. But my first impression is- FANTASTIC idea. As I read *She Matters*, I kept thinking, maybe it's just because I am a writer, too, but I felt like everyone who read this book would be imagining what friends they would include in *their* friendship memoir. I felt like I wanted to get right to work on my own book about all my friends! I think your idea is perfect. It is original, interesting, and I think it will draw people in!

From Jessica to Stephanie:

What do you think about titles for the series? I'm terrible at this sort of thing. I wouldn't want it to be too cheesy or Hallmark sounding.

From Stephanie to Jessica:

As for the title, I'm going to just word vomit at you for a second. Hope that's ok. Throwing out a few ideas: The Girlfriend Series, The Friendship Series, The Friendship Letters, (or take out the word "the") Her Story: Tales of Friendship, (or HerStory- like history, get it? ☺) Girlfriends: Ties That Bind

From Jessica to Stephanie:

I like your titles! How about HerStories: Tales of Friendship?

As we got further into our project, we naturally began to reveal more information about our real lives: which time zone we lived in; our educational backgrounds; the ages of our children. We went through the "getting to know each other" stage of friendship that always feels so much like dating- both invigorating and nerve- wracking.

Jessica to Stephanie:

> Wow, Steph! I didn't realize at first that you worked outside the home too.... I'm so impressed that you have an amazing blog, two kids, read so much, AND have a job!!! So how about this series? I think we're ready to start. Do you think you could "host" the first piece, as soon as you can?

Stephanie to Jessica:

> I am so excited I feel like jumping up and down! (OK, fine there was a little bit of actual jumping involved) I will post live at 8:00 MST tonight. It occurred to me that I have no idea where you live. 😊

Jessica to Stephanie:

> Oh, I'm in Buffalo, New York. I lived in Boston (mostly) since after college, where my husband and I met and got married and I finished my doctoral program, and we moved to Buffalo last year. So I'm in Eastern Standard Time (even though Buffalo is basically the Midwest). Okay, I'm off to try to get a toddler off to bed, who hasn't gotten the memo about Daylight Savings Time....

We went through the phase where we exchanged compliments, reinforcing our appreciation of one another's attributes and providing that essential validation that helps to feed the bonds of friendship.

Jessica to Stephanie:

Oh, and Steph, I just want to tell you that I LOVE working with you... You're fun, level-headed, flexible, smart, and an outstanding writer. And I'm so glad that we "click" on so many things.

Stephanie to Jessica:

Thanks so much for your kind words- I really appreciate it! I think you are an excellent writer, and your intelligence and focus comes through so clearly in everything you write. I really think we make a great team and I echo your sentiments- I am really enjoying working with you!

It wasn't long before we were trading tales of toddler horror, lamenting our unproductive days with ill children, and empathizing with each other's public meltdowns, travel disasters, and sleepless nights.

Stephanie to Jessica:

I haven't even gotten to read the stuff yet- my daughter has totally thwarted all of my plans with her terrible lack of nap due to cold, cough, and teething. ARGH! I have gotten nothing done this afternoon, and the kitchen floor is covered with a horrifying, sticky combination of the milk and Benadryl that were spilled within minutes of each other this morning. Sigh. One of those days.

Jessica to Stephanie:

There must be something in the air with toddlers. Mine did not nap today either. He pooped twice. Yes, TWICE, during nap time. Then it was all over. Today just felt like one of those days that I just want to hit "do over. Bedtime may be 6:15.

Jessica to Stephanie:

> Okay. I'm off. My husband and I are having our first "date"
> tonight in several months. Yeah!

Stephanie to Jessica:

> Yippee- enjoy your date! That is wonderful!

We slowly began to bring a deeper element of honesty into our
correspondence, sharing our career frustrations, insecurities, and struggle
for balance.

Jessica to Stephanie:

> Honestly, Steph, how in the world do you do it? (That's not
> a rhetorical question... Literally, HOW do you do it?) You are
> so on top of things for blogging, and I feel like I'm barely
> getting anything done! And you have a job! I will paint you
> an ugly picture here of the last few days: toddler son hanging
> on my leg for 12 hours a day while I desperately try to check
> my iPhone. Whenever I get near the computer or my phone,
> my son screams, "No!" And he didn't nap yesterday or today.
> And my husband has been working long hours. My son will
> hopefully be back in preschool tomorrow morning (he just has
> a cold, is feeling okay, but has a mild fever so he can't go to
> school).

Stephanie to Jessica:

> As for how I do it all? Let me tell you: I do it badly. I do it
> gracelessly. I am flustered, frenetic, and frazzled. I am fortunate
> in a lot of ways- I only work mornings, and three days a week
> my toddler is in daycare ALL day. (I am writing a post about
> why this works well for us next week- stay tuned.) That means-
> three afternoons a week I have all to myself, and the other
> days, I pretty much spend all of her nap time typing frantically.

241

When I am not alone, I am obsessively sneaking glances at my phone and quickly typing responses to things or jotting down an idea for something to write in my notebook. It is hectic and chaotic. Here is what has suffered- I do not keep my house as clean as I could. (One reason I loved your post last week!) I do not read as much as I'd like. I don't meditate or even veg in front of the TV with my free time. When I see friends during these free patches of time, I feel like rushing so I can get back home to my computer. I am always "on."

Our visions for the project began to grow; our emails were sprinkled with frantic details about our website and publishing process amidst lighthearted banter and serious planning.

Stephanie to Jessica:

One of these days I promise to reply only ONCE to your email, and not with an "Oh, one more thing!" addendum. But today is not that day.

Jessica to Stephanie:

Someone suggested that we think about collecting the friendship stories into an anthology someday and publish them in an e-book. I had been thinking the same thing. I think that if we build up enough essays, and supplement them with our own stories, articles, and maybe even interviews, we would have a great idea for a book.

Stephanie to Jessica:

Here's the short answer- I think that is a fantastic idea. I love it, actually! I think the partnership thing will be a great strength for us. I also think you and I should probably just talk on the phone at some point, don't you? Baby crying- gotta go.

And a book was born.

Acknowlegements

There are quite a lot of people who helped us in many ways with this project.

First, we want to thank our husbands and our families, for their eternal patience, support, and sacrifice.

We also want to thank our "real life" and online friends. Without you, this book wouldn't have happened. A few that we'd like to give special acknowledgement: Deb, Sarah, Lauren, Nina, the moms from the HerStories FB Group, Kathy, JD, and (of course) Jill.

Julie DeNeen, and her "fabulous" blogging knowledge, helped us with much-needed technical assistance during every phase of this project.

Our cover designer, Vanessa of Vanessa No Heart Designs, was infinitely patient with our ever-changing cover vision.

Emily Tedeschi provided copyediting assistance and the support of a great friend.

Norine Dworkin-McDaniel guided us through the world of book launches and marketing.

About the Editors

Jessica Smock is a writer, educator, former teacher, researcher, and mom to a toddler son who lives in Buffalo, New York. She earned her doctorate in educational policy from Boston University last spring after more than a decade as a middle school teacher and curriculum coordinator. She is a graduate of Wesleyan University and wrote her thesis on the transition to first-time motherhood. She writes about parenting, education, and books at her blog School of Smock and at the Huffington Post.

Stephanie Sprenger is a freelance writer, music therapist, and mother of two young daughters. She writes about the imperfect reality of life with kids at her blog, Mommy, for Real. Her work has been featured on various websites, including Mamalode, In the Powder Room, BlogHer, and Scary Mommy. Stephanie performed in the Denver production of Listen To Your Mother in May 2013.

Visit **www.HerStoriesProject.com** to learn more about the editors, contributors, and the project.